Canada's

Intellectual Property Law

in a Nutshell

Martin P.J. Kratz

CARSWELL
Thomson Professional Publishing

This publication is not engaged in rendering legal, accounting or other professional advice. If legal advice or other expert assistance is required, the services of a competent professional should be sought. The analysis contained herein represents the opinions of the authors and should in no way be construed as being official or unofficial policy of any governmental body.

Canadian Cataloguing in Publication Data

Kratz, Martin P.J.
    Canada's intellectual property law in a nutshell

Includes bibliographical references and index.
ISBN 0-459-25478-2

1. Intellectual property — Canada. I. Title.

KE2779.K73 1998   346.7104'8   C98-930546-5
KF2979.K73 1998

The paper used in this publication meets the minimum requirements of the American National Standard for Information Sciences — Permanence of Paper for Printed Library Materials, ANSI X39.48-1984.

 **CARSWELL**
Thomson Professional Publishing

One Corporate Plaza
2075 Kennedy Road
Scarborough, Ontario
M1T 3V4

Customer Service:
Toronto 1-416-609-3800
Elsewhere in Canada/U.S. 1-800-387-5164
Fax 1-416-298-5082

Acknowledgments

This book was written to serve a need for an introduction to the increasingly important and rapidly growing and changing field of industrial and intellectual property law in Canada. The text is intended to provide the reader with a quick introduction to the types of rights protected and important threshold issues such as term of protection and ownership. As well the text introduces special issues and topics but in a manner appropriate for the general reader. One theme underlying the text is the ability to obtain protection of both engineering and scientific and traditional artistic forms of creativity.

The text itself was written using WordPerfect 3.1 on a PowerMac 6400/200. You can send me feedback at mpjk@bjv.ca.

I am grateful to my children, Marcus, Alexandra and Robert, for giving me the time to complete the writing. I am especially grateful for (my wife) Christina's support and encouragement as I worked on "yet another book".

Table of Contents

Table of Cases

[All cases are referenced to page numbers of the text.]

1

What Is Intellectual Property?

1. Introduction

This book serves as an introduction to the evolving field of law known as intellectual property law. It will provide the reader with a useful overview and introduce some of the nuances unique to this complex field. References for additional study are identified throughout the text and in the bibliography.

Intellectual property is not "smart" property, rather, it is property created through human intellect or creativity. Like any other type of property, intellectual property gives the owner certain unique rights which are limited, mitigated or subject to certain exceptions based on economic and public policy factors. Intellectual property rights may define conduct only the owner (or the owner's licensee) may carry out lawfully. In some cases those exclusive rights will result in the creation of a monopoly exercisable by the owner.

The law protecting such creative activity is fragmented between a number of systems involving statutory and/or common law rights. The protection available for a creative work depends, among other things, on how the creativity is expressed and whether or not it is primarily manifested in something that appeals to the eye or in something that is useful.

Because creativity often results in things or manifests itself in ways never before seen or known to mankind, the law may not have contemplated some of the unique issues or situations which may arise from the particular creative act. Further, since at least ten different statutory and/or common law systems may apply, there is bound to be both overlap and gaps in protection available. The purpose of this text is to guide the reader through a basic understanding of these issues and how they may impact particular types of creativity.

2. Tangible and Intangible Manifestations

Intellectual property rights are intangible and must be distinguished from the resultant thing or materials created. It is important to differentiate between the intellectual property right, which is intangible, and the object or thing representing the application of the creativity. That thing or object is generally tangible but need not be so.

For example, an author may write a book and thereby create a copyright owned by the author. When you or I purchase that book we do not acquire any part of the copyright ownership. We may read the book, sell it or give it away to a friend but we may not infringe any of the sole rights of the copyright holder. A similar situation occurs in respect of the engineering plans for a new product design. The product design might be an invention and protectable under patent law. The purchaser of the product acquires no rights in the invention.[1]

If the manifestation of the author's creativity is intangible, such as in the case of the source code of a computer program, the result is the same. Mere access to a copy of the source code does not give a user any part of the copyright ownership of the computer program. Here both the source code and the intellectual property are intangible but that does not mean they are or will become the same thing or that they are exchangeable for each other.

Distinctions between tangible and intangible rights are important for several reasons. Dealings regarding ownership or other rights in an intellectual property right must be expressly stated. Further, in many cases the ownership rules do not always apply in a manner which one might intuitively expect. In many informal arrangements dealing with the creation of new technology or creativity, this may lead to the underlying intellectual property rights being held by the creator. Had the parties anticipated this issue, this may not have been their intent. In such cases it is important to address the intangible rights as well as the rights in the tangible object, technology or work.

3. Types of Monopolies under Intellectual Property

Intellectual property rights give the owner certain sole or exclusive rights to do certain things and to prohibit others from doing such actions. Each form of intellectual property gives rise to certain exclusive rights or conduct. For example, under patent law very substantial monopoly rights are created. The patent owner has the sole right to use, make or sell a product or process embodying the invention. These rights apply against anyone in Canada. There are only a few narrow exceptions permitted under patent law.

---

[1]   See, however, the exhaustion of certain of the rights under patent law discussed in Chapter 12.

In other cases, copyright for example, the owner has a negative monopoly right - the owner has sole rights and can prevent someone from carrying out certain acts. For example, the copyright owner has the sole right to reproduce or publish the work. Yet the copyright owner's rights are not absolute. An independent creator of the same work is unrestrained. Further, copyright law provides an extensive list of exceptions to the sole exercise of the rights of the copyright owner.

Exercise of the monopoly or of other rights arising under intellectual property law are subject to scrutiny under the *Competition Act.*[2] Such intellectual property rights create permissible monopolies or exclusive conduct which, if exercised within the scope provided by the applicable intellectual property law, are not a violation of the provisions of the Act.

4. Why Permit Such Monopoly Rights?

The sole or exclusive rights associated with intellectual property rights are justified on a number of grounds. It is suggested that creators need some protection for the investment made in their creative conduct or they would no longer wish to make such investment with a resulting loss to all society. For example, if an inventor spends considerable time, money and effort on making an invention, the inventor will typically need to recover that investment from commercialization of the invention. If anyone could merely copy the invention, a product based on the invention could be sold at a lower cost (since no creative investment needs to be recovered). The inventor would soon be unable to sell such products and would be dissuaded from making further investment in inventive conduct.

For example, in the biotechnology industry, the rapid growth in investment has resulted in discoveries which can be directly related to the availability of patent protection for these substantial investments. The ability to protect the technology has led to the availability of many new therapies for mankind. If others are permitted to become "free riders" adopting the fruits of another's substantial efforts, then there is a real risk that such research investments and efforts would end and the benefits of the resulting technological advancement would rapidly decrease. More inventors would keep their advances secret and the spread of these benefits would be restricted.

Maintenance of intellectual property rights have been aided by historical factors. Canada inherited many of its intellectual property systems from its imperial parent. In some cases, some of those systems have seen little legislative attention and are in some cases (industrial design law, for example) still closely tied to the historical antecedent legislation.

---

[2]   R.S.C. 1985, c. C-34, ss. 32, 61(1), 78(5). See also the defences or limits described in relation to each applicable system of intellectual property law.

Canada is a trading nation and has signed numerous international treaties guaranteeing intellectual property rights to nationals of other treaty countries. In order for Canadians to benefit from the protection available in such other countries, Canada must also provide applicable protection. These arrangements were most recently confirmed with the adoption of the Trade Related Aspects of Intellectual Property Rights Agreement as part of the Uruguay Round of Multilateral Trade Negotiations.[3]

5. Artistic and Utilitarian Creativity

Intellectual property rights are not available for all types of creative expression despite the effort, cost and investment involved in the creative process. Economic and historical factors dominate the form and extent of protection available for specific forms of creativity.

Creativity expressed in the traditional humanities (such as art or literature) generally finds protection without formality or cost and regardless of the effort involved in making the work (for example, under copyright law). By contrast, creativity expressed in subjects of engineering or the sciences (such as useful designs or inventions) generally finds the main prospects for protection available only under patent law. This system of law only provides protection for substantial and significant advances over prior technology.[4] By contrast, useful features are not protectable under many other systems of law.[5] This may result in little or no available protection for creativity which does not meet the high standard required for patent protection.

Yet a simplistic analysis is inadequate. Computer programs may be useful and, since they are protected under copyright law as literary works, the form of the computer program receives the same protection advantages as a book. An international consensus adopted copyright as a form of protection for computer programs and Canada has followed that lead.

However, fundamentally, and in most cases, creativity expressed in useful things which do not meet the high level of creativity required under patent law are unprotected in Canada.

---

[3]   For more details see Chapter 14, "International Treaties". See also, Final Act Embodying the Results of the Uruguay Round of Multilateral Trade Negotiations, done at Marrakech, Morocco, April 15, 1994, Annex 1C: Agreement on Trade-Related Aspects of Intellectual Property Rights, April 15, 1994. This treaty set minimum standards for the level of intellectual property protection to be provided by member countries.

[4]   See Chapter 12, "Patents".

[5]   See, for example, *Copyright Act*, R.S.C. 1985, c. C-42, s. 64(3), and *Industrial Design Act*, R.S.C. 1985, c. I-9, s. 5(1), which limit protection available for utilitarian functions of designs. Canada also provides no protection for utility models: see Chapter 13.

6. Interaction between Forms of Intellectual Property

Several intellectual property rights may apply to a single expression of creativity. One should thoroughly review the potential applicability of *each form* of intellectual property protection to a particular creative expression or technology under study. Overlapping protection is likely in many cases. The introductory text and the last section of most chapters in this book provides a description of some of these interactions.

For example, the form of a computer program would be protectable as a literary work under copyright law. Similarly, screen displays, logos or characters generated by a computer program may be protected as artistic works under copyright law. The programmer will have moral rights arising from his or her efforts in writing the program. The algorithm underlying a computer program may be an invention and protectable under patent law. It is also typically maintained as confidential information. The computer program may itself be known in its marketplace by a unique name, logo or symbol - in relation to which trademark rights may arise. Each of these rights (other than the moral rights) may be enjoyed by the owner. Each of these rights must be observed by the user of the computer program. Each of these rights may give the owner rights against a pirate.

An important early step is to properly characterize the work, device, process or thing being studied for protection. Once the technology or creative expression is properly characterized, then the nature of the protection available may be determined. Examples of characterization may be found in the Canada Practice Guides, *Protection of Copyright and Industrial Design* and *Obtaining Patents.*[6]

7. Dealings with Intellectual Property Rights

With some exceptions and unique issues, most legal systems in Canada providing protection for different types of intellectual property provide that licences or assignments of the rights are permitted. In most cases an assignment must expressly deal with the applicable rights and must be in writing.[7] In many cases assignments and licences must be registered in the applicable government registry in order to be enforceable against third parties.

The ownership rules may give rise to unexpected results if ignored in the creation of new works or technology. Particularly in the case of things protected by copyright, informal arrangements dealing with the creation of new works may lead to the underlying intellectual property rights being held by the creator when the work leading to that creative activity was funded by and at the direction of another person. This may be contrary to what the

---

[6]   Practice Guide (Toronto: Carswell, 1995).

[7]   See, for example, *Copyright Act*, R.S.C. 1985, c. C-42, s. 13(4), *Patent Act*, R.S.C. 1985, c. P-4, s. 50(1), (2), but see *Trade-marks Act*, R.S.C. 1985, c. T-13, s. 48.

contracting party expected to get. In such cases it is important to address the intellectual property rights of the parties expressly.

Bankruptcy law[8] and other law[9] provide unique rules applicable to certain intellectual property rights. Some of the systems of intellectual property are in need of reform and modernization (industrial design law, for example) and present provisions may provide traps for the unwary. For example, in order to enhance rights available, some of the systems require marking of certain specific forms of notices on an article or thing made using the creative design.

The reader should note that many dealings with intellectual property rights are complex. The reader is encouraged to consult detailed references or seek professional counsel when warranted.

---

[8]   See, for example, *Bankruptcy and Insolvency Act*, R.S.C. 1985, c. B-3, s. 83.

[9]   See, for example, provisions of the *Bills of Exchange Act*, R.S.C. 1985, c. B-4, which require certain formal requirements in respect of payments made in relation to patent assignments.

2

Copyright Law

1. Introduction

Copyright protects the form in which literary, artistic, musical and dramatic works may be expressed. Copyright law is very pervasive and applies to many forms in which creativity is expressed. Unlike patent or industrial design law, copyright arises automatically upon the creation of an original work that is fixed in a tangible form.

Copyright arose – at least in relation to Canada's English legal heritage – during the middle ages as a system of law to protect publishers' rights and evolved to become a system of law providing a framework of authors' rights. Over the years copyright law has expanded to cover new forms of creativity (called "works" under copyright law), for example, phonographs and more recently, computer programs, performances, rights in satellite transmissions and rental of sound recordings. Copyright law continues to evolve and provide a broad form of protection for many works.

Specific forms of protection for so-called moral rights of authors[1] and rights of performers and others arise under the *Copyright Act*, R.S.C. 1985, c. C-42.[2] Modern copyright law provides for a delicate balance of rights between creators and users. As a result one may look at the *Copyright Act* as both a system of intellectual property law and also as economic legislation providing a framework[3] and governing numerous creative industries and implementing

---

[1]   See Chapter 3.

[2]   See Chapter 4, "Neighbouring Rights". Note that all future footnote references to the *Copyright Act* will be indicated by "CA" following the section number. For an electronic version of the Act, see <http://xinfo.ic.gc.ca/>.

[3]   See, for example, extensive provisions regulating the broadcast, cable and satellite business in the *Copyright Act*.

Parliament's social policy objectives.[4] Copyright law also has grown to play a role in addressing some forms of unfair competition accommodating the fact that Canada has not developed an unfair competition tort such as that developed in the United States.[5]

Copyright is an intangible right separate and apart from the work which is the subject of copyright protection. It is important to distinguish between the rights of copyright and other rights, such as possession. Possession of a work protected by copyright (*i.e.*, this book) may allow the possessor to use the work in many ways but the possessor is not permitted to make copies of the work (or otherwise carry out any of the conduct solely reserved to the copyright owner). It is therefore common that one person or entity will own the copyright to the work and another distinct person or entity has possession or use of a copy of the work. An example of this situation is found with books – the author or publisher may own the copyright in the book (giving the copyright holder a variety of rights) and copies of the book may be owned by many others. The book owner has the right to read (or use) the book, to discard it, to sell it to another, to give it away – but may not violate the rights of the copyright owner (including new rights to control parallel importation of new and some used books).[6]

Copyright law provides a number of substantial rights which provide a degree of protection over the *form* in which concepts or ideas may be expressed. As a general rule, copyright law does not protect ideas or concepts themselves. For example, in the case of computer programs, copyright law protects the form in which the instructions are set out. In the case of a book,

---

[4]   For example, note the availability of certain educational exemptions to "non-profit" educational institutions presumably to favour these institutions over private schools. There appears to be no copyright rationale to suggest that the educational uses would be different between private or non-profit educational institutions. As a result this suggests Parliament is implementing social policy. See *An Act to Amend the Copyright Act*, S.C. 1997, c. 24.

[5]   An important example of this difference is seen in Canada's protection, under copyright law, for physical and electronic databases, using the "sweat of the brow" principle, (*i.e.*, rewarding the collection and selection effort with protection) whereas the American courts have applied narrower copyright principles to address copying of another's databases. Contrast the results in *Feist Publications, Inc. v. Rural Telephone Service Co.*, 111 S. Ct. 1282 (U.S. 1991); *B.C. Jockey Club v. Standen (Winbar Publications)* (1983), 73 C.P.R. (2d) 164 (B.C. S.C.), affd (1985), 8 C.P.R. (3d) 283 (B.C. C.A.); and *L'Index Téléphonique (N.L.) de notre localité v. Imprimerie Garceau Ltée* (1987), 18 C.I.P.R. 133 (Que. S.C.). See also comments in Siebrasse, "Copyright in Facts and Information" 11 C.I.P.R. 191. See, however, the recent case of *Tele-Direct (Publications) Inc. v. American Business Information Inc.* (1996), 74 C.P.R. (3d) 72 (Fed. T.D.) which suggests some Canadian courts may be departing from this "sweat of the brow" approach, at least in relation to computer databases.

[6]   See changes introduced in *An Act to amend the Copyright Act*, S.C. 1997, c. 24.

copyright protects the phrases used to express the plot but not the broad concepts underlying that plot. In another example, a method of teaching mathematics using coloured rods is not protected by the copyright in a book describing the method.[7]

A common view is that the basis for the law of copyright is that the protection of the author's economic rights and interests, such as, the protection of the right to copy, will encourage individual artistic and creative activity and will permit the author to benefit from the rewards of creation.

Copyright has changed considerably in recent years and can be expected to continue to change and expand. The development of new technology and the economic factors of control over certain types of conduct have been a major force in the development of the law of copyright – both in the infancy of copyright and now when satellite transmission, interactive computer design or graphics, music sampling and other developments continue to create pressure for legal protection of new forms of works.

Copyright, in Canada, exists solely under the *Copyright Act*.[8] The federal Parliament has exclusive jurisdiction over the field of copyright.[9] Prior to confederation there existed a common law doctrine of copyright. Parliament, in exercising its exclusive jurisdiction, has completely occupied the field.[10] The rights under copyright are statutory rights.[11]

---

[7]   *Cuisenaire v. South West Imports Ltd.*, [1969] S.C.R. 208.

[8]   Note that as of the writing of this text the long-awaited phase two of copyright reform had been introduced into Canadian copyright law as *An Act to amend the Copyright Act*, S.C. 1997, c. 24. The reforms contemplated by this Act have been included in this text. Background on these reforms may be found in the *Charter of Rights for Creators*, Government of Canada, 1985 and the subsequent governmental reports, position papers and minutes of committee hearings both for that legislation as well as for S.C. 1988, c. 65 – the so-called "phase one" of copyright reform.

[9]   See *Constitution Act, 1982*, being Schedule B of the *Canada Act, 1982* (U.K.), 1982, c. 11, s. 91(23).

[10]   The statutory nature of the copyright was provided by s. 89 (CA) former s. 63 (CA), which stated: "No person is entitled to copyright or any similar right in any literary, dramatic, musical or artistic work otherwise than under and in accordance with this Act, or of any other statutory enactment for the time being in force, but nothing in this section shall be construed as abrogating any right or jurisdiction to restrain a breach of trust or confidence." The latter words of s. 89 implicitly recognize that the right of copyright co-exists with the law of trade secrets.

[11]   See *Compo Co. v. Blue Crest Music Inc.*, [1980] 1 S.C.R. 357, 45 C.P.R. (2d) 1, 105 D.L.R. (3d) 249, which held that rights under copyright law are statutory rights. See also *Apple Computer Inc. v. Mackintosh Computers Ltd.* (1986), 8 C.I.P.R. 153, 28 D.L.R. (4th) 178 (Fed. T.D.), vard (1987), 16 C.I.P.R. 15 (Fed. C.A.), affd (1990), 71 D.L.R. (4th) 95 (S.C.C.) where the Court held that a taking or use of a work was only actionable if it was contrary to rights provided under the *Copyright Act*.

A primary advantage of copyright protection is the automatic creation of enforceable rights. There are several advantages to protection under the copyright system. The *Copyright Act* gives the copyright holder a right *in rem*, a right against all the world, to prevent appropriation of certain of the labours of one author by another. This, like patent law, allows one to enforce rights against strangers, persons one might not have any other dealings with. This is an important advantage over contractual and trade secret protection which may protect only against wrongdoing between specific parties who have an *existing* relationship.

2. Scope of Rights

Copyright provides a bundle of enforceable rights to the copyright owner. Copyright consists of a number of rights each of significance to various industries. These rights provide a negative monopoly right for the owner of the copyright.[12]

Subject to the exemptions provided by the *Copyright Act*, the copyright owner is able to either authorize or exclude others from certain activity enumerated in s. 3(1)[13] and other provisions. These provide for the following

---

[12]   For internet issues involving copyright, see Gahtan, Kratz, Mann, *Internet Law*, (Carswell, 1998).

[13]   Subsection 3(1) (CA) states:

> For the purposes of this Act "copyright", in relation to a work, means the sole right to produce or reproduce the work or any substantial part thereof in any material form whatever, to perform the work or any substantial part thereof in public or, if the work is unpublished, to publish the work or any substantial part thereof, and includes the sole right
>
> (*a*) to produce, reproduce, perform, or publish any translation of the work,
>
> (*b*) in the case of a dramatic work, to convert it into a novel or other non-dramatic work,
>
> (*c*) in the case of a novel or other non-dramatic work, or of an artistic work, to convert it into a dramatic work, by way of performance in public or otherwise,
>
> (*d*) in the case of a literary, dramatic or musical work, to make any sound recording, cinematograph film or other contrivance by means of which the work may be mechanically reproduced or performed,
>
> (*e*) in the case of any literary, dramatic, musical or artistic work, to reproduce, adapt and publicly present the work as a cinematographic work,
>
> (*f*) in the case of any literary, dramatic, musical or artistic work, to communicate the work to the public by telecommunication,
>
> (*g*) to present in a public exhibition, for the purpose other than sale or hire, an artistic work created after June 7, 1988, other than a map, chart or plan,
>
> (*h*) in the case of a computer program that can be reproduced in the ordinary course of its use, other than by reproduction during its execution in conjunction with a

specific rights and, in each case below, the copyright owner also has the right to authorize any such acts.

(a) Reproduction Right

The copyright owner has the sole right to reproduce the work or any substantial part thereof in any material form whatever.[14] This provision gives the owner of the performer's right a degree of control over unauthorized copies of, for example, a computer program, building or engineering plans, a song or a book.[15]

(b) Production Right

The copyright owner has the sole right to produce the work or any substantial part thereof in any material form whatever.[16] This provision gives the owner of the performer's right a degree of control over the making of, for example, copies of a dramatic work.

(c) Public Performance Right

The copyright owner has the sole right to perform, or in the case of a lecture to deliver, the work or any substantial part thereof in public.[17] This provision gives the owner of the public performance right control over unauthorized performance of, for example, a musical work (*e.g.*, a song) in public.[18] In addition, copyright is deemed to be infringed by any person who for his private profit permits a theatre or other place of entertainment to be used for the public performance of the work without the consent of the owner

---

machine, device or computer, to rent out the computer program, and to authorize any such acts, and

(*i*) in the case of a musical work, to rent out a sound recording in which the work is embodied.

[14]   See s. 3(1) (CA).

[15]   See, for example, *University of London Press Ltd. v. University Tutorial Press Ltd.*, [1916] 2 Ch. 601: copying examinations; *Football League Ltd. v. Littlewoods Pools Ltd.*, [1959] 1 Ch. 637, [1959] 2 All E.R. 546 (U.K.): copying a schedule of games of a professional sporting association; and *Apple Computer Inc. v. Mackintosh Computers Ltd.* (1986), 8 C.I.P.R. 153, 28 D.L.R. (4th) 178 (Fed. T.D.), vard (1987), 16 C.I.P.R. 15 (Fed. C.A.), affd (1990), 71 D.L.R. (4th) 95 (S.C.C.): copying machine readable versions of a computer program.

[16]   See s. 3(1) (CA).

[17]   See s. 3(1) (CA).

[18]   For example, in *Canadian Admiral Corp. v. Rediffusion Inc.*, [1954] Ex. C.R. 382 (Ex. Ct.), the Court dealt with the issue of the ability of the owner of rights to televise professional football games to control subsequent public performance of those games.

of the copyright, unless that person was not aware, and had no reasonable ground for suspecting, that the performance would be an infringement of copyright.[19]

(d) Publication Right

The copyright owner has the sole right, if the work is unpublished, to publish the work or any substantial part thereof.[20] This provision gives the owner of the publication right the ability to control when an unpublished manuscript is released to the public. In *Re Dickens*[21] this right was held by one ultimate beneficiary of Charles Dickens' will while the physical property in an unpublished manuscript was held by a second beneficiary under that will.[22]

(e) Translation Right

The copyright owner has the sole right to produce, reproduce, perform, or publish any translation of the work.[23] This provision gives the owner of the performer's right the ability to control the making of unauthorized translations of, for example, a book.[24]

(f) Adaptation Right

The copyright owner has the sole right in the case of a dramatic work, to convert it into a novel or other non-dramatic work,[25] or in the case of a novel or other non-dramatic work, or of an artistic work, to convert it into a dramatic work, by way of performance in public or otherwise.[26] These provisions give the owner of the performer's right the ability to control unauthorized adaptation of certain types of works from one form into another.

---

[19]   These further rights are provided by s. 27(5) (CA).

[20]   See s. 3(1) (CA).

[21]   [1935] 1 Ch. 267 (U.K. C.A.). See also *Dawson v. Hill* (1934), 152 L.T. 375 (U.K. C.A.).

[22]   As a result neither could publish the work — one had the rights to publish but no manuscript and the other had the manuscript but no right to publish. Note that S.C. 1997, c. 24 limits the term of copyright in such unpublished works. See Section 8, "Term of Protection", *infra*, for more details.

[23]   See s. 3(1)(*a*) (CA).

[24]   The issue of whether a copy of a computer program in a different computer language is a translation under the *Copyright Act* has received some judicial consideration. In *Apple Computer Inc. v. Mackintosh Computers Ltd.* (1986), 8 C.I.P.R. 153, 28 D.L.R. (4th) 178 (Fed. T.D.), vard (1987), 16 C.I.P.R. 15 (Fed. C.A.), affd (1990), 71 D.L.R. (4th) 95 (S.C.C.), the trial judge found a translation to exist, some justices of the Court of Appeal found no translation and the Supreme Court did not need to rule on the issue.

[25]   See s. 3(1)(*b*) (CA).

[26]   See s. 3(1)(*c*) (CA).

For example, the copyright owner of a book (a literary work) has the right to adapt the book into a movie (a dramatic work).

(g) Mechanical Reproduction Right

The copyright owner has the sole right in the case of a literary, dramatic or musical work, to make any sound recording, cinematograph film or other contrivance by means of which the work may be mechanically performed or delivered.[27] Modern copyright law replaced the concept of "record, perforated roll, cinematographic film or other contrivance by means of which the work may be mechanically performed or delivered" with the concept of a "sound recording" or cinematographic recording of a work by means of which the work may be mechanically performed.[28]

The law gives the owner of the mechanical reproduction right control over making unauthorized copies of, for example, a compact disk (CD) which contains a musical work.[29] In addition, the owner of copyright in respect of any sound recording has the sole right to rent it out. This provision gives the owner of the copyright in a mechanical contrivance (*e.g.*, a CD) control over others providing copies of the CD to others under rental arrangements. (See also Chapter 4, "Neighbouring Rights", which provides that performers have certain rights in respect of the mechanical reproduction of their performances.)

(h) Cinematographic Presentation Right

The copyright owner has the sole right in the case of any literary, dramatic, musical or artistic work, to reproduce, adapt and publicly present the work by cinematograph.[30] This provision gives the owner of the performer's right control over unauthorized presentation of a work to the public by cinematograph.

(i) Communication Right

The copyright owner has the sole right in the case of any literary, dramatic, musical or artistic work, to communicate the work to the public by telecommunication.[31] This provision gives the owner of this right a degree of

---

[27]   See s. 3(1)(*d*) (CA).

[28]   See s. 3(1)(*d*) (CA).

[29]   Note, however, that having a licence to make a public performance of a work does not imply any licence or right to make a mechanical reproduction of a work for the purpose of exercising the right to perform the work in public: see *Bishop v. Stevens*, [1990] 2 S.C.R. 467.

[30]   See s. 3(1)(*e*) (CA).

[31]   See s. 3(1)(*f*) (CA).

control over unauthorized transmission of, for example, a musical work to the public through use of any means of telecommunications. In order to avoid uncertainty, persons who occupy apartments, hotel rooms or dwelling units situated in the same building are part of the public and a communication intended to be received exclusively by such persons is a communication to the public.[32] As further clarification, if a person's only role is to provide the telecommunication means necessary to communicate the work to the public the person does not by that act alone communicate the work to the public.[33]

Modern copyright law provides for a new communication right in respect of a communication signal[34] and provides that the broadcaster has a copyright in the communication signal that is broadcast. This right gives the broadcaster the right to fix the broadcast, reproduce a fixed copy of the broadcast, perform a television communication signal to the public on payment of entrance fees, to authorize retransmission of the communication signal and to authorize any of these sole rights.[35]

(j) Exhibition Right

The copyright owner has the sole right to present in a public exhibition, for the purpose other than sale or hire, an artistic work created after June 7, 1988, other than a map, chart or plan.[36] This provision gives the owner of the copyright in artistic works (for example, a painting, engraving or photograph) control over any unauthorized display of the artistic work in a public place except for the purpose of sale or rental. This right should be reviewed by any artist and/or art collector.[37]

---

[32]   See s. 2.4 (CA) [note: this issue formerly dealt with in s. 14.01(2)]. This provision mirrors s. 1.2 respecting exercise of the communication rights of the copyright holder under s. 3(1)(*f*). These provisions overcome the problems arising from the decision in *Canadian Admiral Corp. v. Rediffusion Inc.*, [1954] Ex. C.R. 382 (Ex. Ct.), which held that a cable transmission to individual dwelling units was not a communication to the public. See also the definitions of "performance" and "compilations" in s. 2.

[33]   See s. 2.3 (CA), former s. 14.01(3) (CA). This provision mirrors s. 3(1.3), which related to the copyright holder's exercise of the communication right under s. 3(1)(*f*). These provisions reinforce the decision of the Supreme Court of Canada in *C.A.P.A.C. v. CTV (Television) Network*, [1968] S.C.R. 676, 55 C.P.R. 132, 68 D.L.R. (2d) 98, which found that a microwave transmission of a television signal, including musical works, was not a communication to the public of the musical works by the microwave facility operator.

[34]   Basically radio frequency waves transmitted for reception by the public without the benefit of an artificial guide.

[35]   See Chapter 4, "Neighbouring Rights", for more details on such rights.

[36]   See s. 3(1)(*g*) (CA).

[37]   See Chapter 3, "Moral Rights", for other issues applicable to the display of artistic works.

(k) Rental Rights

Copyright law provides rental rights for sound recordings and computer programs as mechanisms to manage the access to these works with adequate compensation to the authors. These provisions give the owner of the copyright control over others providing copies of the computer program or sound recording to others under rental arrangements.

In the case of a musical work the copyright owner has the right to rent out a sound recording of a musical work.[38]

In the case of a computer program that can be reproduced in the ordinary course of its use, other than by reproduction during its execution in conjunction with a machine, device or computer the copyright owner has the sole right to rent out the computer program.[39]

(l) Commercial Action/Importation

Copyright in a work, sound recording, communication signal or fixation of a performer's performance may be infringed by any person who:

(a) sells or rents it out;

(b) distributes copies of it to such an extent as to affect prejudicially the owner of the copyright;

(c) by way of trade exhibits in public, distributes, exposes or offers it for sale.[40]

It is also an infringement of copyright in a work, sound recording, communication signal or fixation of a performer's performance to possess it for the purpose of the above[41] or to import it into Canada for the purpose of the above.[42]

(m) Rights to Control Exclusive Distribution of Books

The copyright owner or an exclusive distributor of books have certain rights to control parallel importation of new and some used copies of the books in Canada.[43]

---

[38]   See s. 3(1)(*i*) (CA).

[39]   See s. 3(1)(*h*) (CA).

[40]   See s. 27(2) (CA).

[41]   See s. 27(2)(*d*) (CA).

[42]   See s. 27(2)(*e*) (CA).

[43]   See s. 27.1 (CA).

(i)   Generally

One should review applicability of all rights under the *Copyright Act* which may apply to the creative activity. The rights of the copyright holder do *not* provide a broad ability to exercise any monopoly over any use of the copyright protected work other than those limits set out in the *Copyright Act* itself. As a result, a purchaser of a book is free to loan or rent that book to others, dispose of it whether by gift, resale or ultimate disposal or destruction.

In addition to the sole rights of the copyright owner, the owner of the copyright also has the right to authorize others to carry out any of the acts contemplated by those sole rights.

It is an infrigement of the copyright in a work if a person, without the consent of the owner of the copyright, does any act that only the copyright owner has the right to do.[44]

3. Limits on Copyright

The *Copyright Act* prohibits the reproduction or public performance of certain works without the permission of the copyright holder. There are numerous exemptions or limitations to a copyright holder's rights. Some substantial defences or limits on copyright are described below.

(a) works which indicate permission to copy, use or perform any other protected activity in relation to the work;[45]

(b) where the copyright holder has given permission for the copying or other activity;[46]

(c) works where the term of copyright (for most cases the life of the author plus the end of the year in which the author dies plus fifty years) has expired;

---

[44]   See s. 27(1) (CA).

[45]   Many works contain a copyright notice or copyright information. See, for example, the copyright page of a book, licence provisions for many computer programs or notices in many films and video presentations. If in doubt, contact the copyright owner.

[46]   Generally it is not difficult to obtain permission from a copyright holder to make copies for non-commercial or non-competitive uses. Most major content providers such as newspapers and media outlets have copyright permissions officers who can assist with any request. The permission should be recorded in writing with a confirming letter providing specifics of the terms of the permission and the works which may be copied or used. If one cannot locate the copyright holder the Copyright Board can, in some circumstances, give the permission to copy.

(d) works created and first published in countries which are not members of copyright treaties with Canada;[47]

(e) under an exemption under the *Copyright Act* (see discussion in Section 4, *infra*);

(f) if a unsubstantial amount is taken;

(g) copyright does not extend to ideas, facts, processes or methods;

(h) copyright does not extend to works in the public domain (for example, if the term of copyright has expired);

(i) copyright does not extend to useful features of a work;[48] or

(j) any action must be brought within three years after expiration of the infringement.[49]

4. Exemptions under the *Copyright Act*

While there are numerous exemptions under the *Copyright Act* most are limited to very specific situations. Some of the most important exemptions under the Act are the fair dealing exemption, the home copying exemption, educational use exemptions and exemptions for libraries, museums and archives. Each of these and some other exemptions are discussed below.

(a) Fair Dealing Exemption

The *Copyright Act* permits copying, without permission of the copyright holder, when such copying constitutes fair dealing with the work (*i.e.*, the conduct is fair or equitable behaviour and has no material adverse commercial impact on the copyright holder).[50] To be exempt, activity must be both fair dealing and within a limited class of permitted exempt activities.

Fair dealing for the purpose of research or private study does not infringe copyright.[51] Fair dealing for the purpose of criticism or review or for the purpose of news reporting or news summary does not infringe copyright if given in the source is the name of the author, performer or maker, (and in the

---

[47] See Chapter 14, "International Treaties", for a discussion of the applicable international treaties. See also *Protection of Copyright and Industrial Designs*, Practice Guide (Toronto: Carswell, 1995) for a review of the operation of these treaty provisions and a listing of treaty members.

[48] Section 64 (CA).

[49] See s. 41 (CA).

[50] See s. 29 (CA).

[51] See s. 29 (CA).

case of news reporting or news summary, the broadcaster, in the case of a communication signal) as applicable, are mentioned.[52]

While little case law exists on this point, a good rule of thumb is that generally less than and no more than one copy of a work may be taken for one of such purposes so long as the taking constitutes fair dealing (*i.e.*, is equitable).

Factors which may be taken into consideration in determining if the conduct is fair dealing include:

(a) the impact of the copying on the copyright owner's economic reward;

(b) the type of work and its purpose; and

(c) the amount and extent of the copying.

(b) Private Copying of Sound Recordings

Modern copyright law seeks to address the issue of widespread reproduction of copyright protected works by various means. One approach is to legitimize the practice of many Canadians to make copies of sound recordings by providing for a home or private copying exemption in relation to the making of copies of sound recordings. A second approach is to facilitate common administration of copyrights by providing for the formation of collectives to hold and manage copyrights for numerous authors.

The home or private copying exemption provides that it is not an infringement of copyright to copy onto an audio recording medium:

(a) a music work in a sound recording;

(b) a performer's performance of a musical work in a sound recording; and

(c) a sound recording in which a musical work or a performer's performance of a musical work is embodied if it is for private use.[53]

This exemption legitimizes the widespread home copying activity present in Canada[54] and provides a means to compensate authors, performers, makers

---

[52]   See s. 29.1 (CA), for the criticism or review exemption and s. 29.2 for the news reporting or news summary exemption.

[53]   See s. 29(2) (CA).

[54]   It also brings Canada closer to being consistent with the United States, at least in so far as musical works are concerned. The United States has a broader "fair use" exemption which permitted some home copying activity. See, for example, *Universal City Studios v. Sony Corp. of America*, 104 S. Ct. 774 (U.S. 1984), in which the United States Supreme Court found that "time shifting" of television programs by copying them was exempt under American copyright law. The private copying exemption will also provide compensation to the rights holders affected.

and other rights holders through the levy of a blank audio media royalty which will be added to all blank audio recording media (presently cassette tapes) sold in Canada. The manufacturer or importer of the blank audio recording media would collect the levy. This levy would then be remitted to the applicable collective[55] on behalf of the eligible author, performer and makers.

It is important to note that the exemption is only available for private use. Copying for commercial purposes, including rental or sale of the copy, would still be infringing. This exemption does not permit any public performance of the copy nor any communication by telecommunication to the public of the copy.[56]

(c) Educational Exemptions

Modern copyright law provides the long-awaited expansion of the exemptions available for educational purposes.[57] These new exemptions provide that it is not an infringement of copyright for an educational institution or a person acting under its authority to make a copy of a work

(a) onto a dry-erase board, flip chart or any other thing on which written material may be displayed, or

(b) as an image projected using an over-head projector or similar device for the purposes of education or training on the premises of an educational institution.[58]

A limited exemption permits certain uses of a work for a purpose related to the giving of an assignment, test or examination on the premises of an educational institution including, but not limited to, setting and

---

[55] A collective is a society or other organization which represents the interests of a large group of copyright holders (whose works make up the "repetour" of the collective"). The existence of collectives facilitates the ability to distribute this new royalty but also provides blanket consents to use of material in the repetour. Rates charged by collectives are established by the Copyright Board. See also s. 83(2) (CA). For more details on the operation of several of the more substantial collectives, see *Protection of Copyright and Industrial Designs*, Practice Guide (Toronto: Carswell, 1995).

[56] For more details of performer's rights see Chapter 4, "Neighbouring Rights".

[57] See s. 27(2)(*d*) (CA) which, before the changes provided by S.C. 1997, c. 24 provided: The "educational exemption" provides that "short passages", from sources in which no copyright subsists from works not intended for use in schools, suitably acknowledged, do not infringe in school use, so long as "not more than two of the passages from works by the same author are published . . . within five years". This was a very limited exemption and of little use to most educational institutions. This exemption is generally preserved in the revised law but supplemented by additional exemptions.

[58] See s. 29.4(1) (CA).

communicating the questions and answers to the persons completing the assignment or taking the test or examination, and answering the questions by those persons.[59]

Limited exemptions also permit the following acts if they are done on the premises of an educational institution for educational or training purposes and not for profit, before an audience consisting primarily of students of the educational institution, instructors acting under the authority of the educational institution or any person who is directly responsible for setting a curriculum for the educational institution:

(a) the live performance in public, primarily by students of the educational institution, of a work;

(b) the performance in public of a sound recording or of a work or performer's performance that is embodied in a sound recording; and

(c) the performance in public of a work or other subject-matter at the time of its communication to the public by telecommunication.[60]

Social studies and teachers of similar subjects obtain certain rights to use current affairs information available through certain news programs. The teacher or other authorized person with an educational institution may

(a) make, at the time of its communication to the public by telecommunication, a single copy of a news program or a news commentary program, for the purposes of performing the copy for the students of the educational institution for educational or training purposes; and

(b) perform the copy in public, at any time or times within one year after the making of a copy under paragraph (a), before an audience consisting primarily of students of the educational institution on its premises for educational or training purposes.[61]

The copy cannot be kept for more than thirty days and royalties may be payable for such use. A complex administrative record-keeping and marking process is imposed on the educational institution as part of the exercise of this exemption.[62]

---

[59]   See s. 29.4(2) (CA).

[60]   See s. 29.5 (CA).

[61]   See s. 29.6(1) (CA). [Note: not yet in force at time of printing.]

[62]   See ss. 29.5-29.9 (CA). [Note: ss. 29.6, 29.7 and 29.9 not yet in force at time of printing.]

(d) Library, Museum and Archive Exemptions

Modern copyright law seeks to solve the problem of liability of innocent intermediaries in making copies for others where those others have the right to make the copies themselves. This problem arises most frequently in the case of libraries where a researcher may wish to make a copy of an article for his or her private study. In most cases, the researcher has the right to make the copy for private study under an existing exemption. In the past, a third party, for example, a university library, would not qualify under the exemption since it was not making the copy for its own private study. This gave rise to possible liability for copyright infringement for the library or intermediary. Note that even with this exemption the libraries or other archival institutions can still be liable for other infringements.[63] Similarly one should note that the intermediate reproduction may also be permissible under some other exemption.[64]

The exemptions provide that it is not an infringement of copyright for a library, archive or museum or a person acting under the authority of such an organization to make for the maintenance or management of its permanent collection or the collection of another library, archive or museum, a copy of a work or other subject-matter, whether published or unpublished, in its permanent collection in certain circumstances.[65]

---

[63] See, for example, *Moorhouse v. University of New South Wales* (1975), 6 A.L.R. 193 (Aust. H.C.), in which a university library was found liable for authorizing infringements resulting from use of photocopiers in the library by third parties. Note that the fair dealing exemption was not raised in this case. This problem is now specifically addressed by s. 30.3 (CA), which provides a limited exemption provided an applicable copyright notice and caution.

[64] See, for example, the case of reproduction of federal crown legal materials which is permitted by the *Reproduction of Federal Law Order,* SI/97-5, (Canada Gazette, Pt. II, Vol. 131, No. 1, p. 44).

[65] See s. 30.1 (CA) [Note: not yet in force at time of printing], which provides such rights in relation to the following situations:

    (*a*)   if the original is rare or published and is

        (i) deteriorating, damaged or lost, or

        (ii) at risk of deterioration or becoming damaged or lost;

    (*b*)   for the purposes of on-site consultation if the original cannot be viewed, handled or listened to because of its condition or because of the atmospheric conditions in which it must be kept;

    (*c*)   in an alternative format if the original is currently in an obsolete format or the technology required to use the original is unavailable;

    (*d*)   for the purposes of internal record-keeping and cataloguing;

    (*e*)   for insurance purposes or police investigations; or

    (*f*)   if necessary for restoration.

(e) Public Policy

In certain cases, public policy appears to permit use of copyright materials in a manner which would otherwise be infringing conduct. Perhaps the best example of this defence or exemption is the use of legal materials, such as statutes, regulations, judges' decisions and similar legal materials in the pursuance of legal processes or activities. This is a case where the broad public policy suggesting that each person is deemed to know the law conflicts with the restrictions available under copyright law.[66] In another case, the House of Lords found there was a public policy exemption in the copyright claim of an automobile manufacturer permitting the making of spare parts.[67]

(f) Other Common Exemptions

Other common exemptions include:[68]

(a) making a copy of a computer program owner by the user for archive purposes only or to adapt the computer program for use on a different computer system;[69]

(b) reproduction of a work for the purposes of either reproduction of certain materials under the *Cultural Property Export and Import Act,* R.S.C. 1985, c. C-51,[70] disclosure under the *Access to Information Act,* R.S.C. 1985, c. A-1 or similar provincial Act,[71] disclosure under the *Privacy Act,* R.S.C. 1985, c. P-21 or similar provincial Act,[72] or the making of a fixation or copy of a work or other copyright subject-matter to comply with the *Broadcasting Act,* R.S.C. 1985, c. B-9;[73]

(c) the incidental and accidental inclusion of a work in another work;[74] and

---

[66]   See, for example, *B.C. Jockey Club v. Standen (Winbar Publications)* (1983), 146 D.L.R. (3d) 693 (B.C. S.C.), affd (1985), 22 D.L.R. (4th) 467 (B.C. C.A.): the Court expressed the view that judicial opinions may be published on public policy grounds.

[67]   See *British Leyland Motor Corp. Ltd. v. Armstrong Patents Co.,* [1986] 1 All E.R. 850, [1986] F.S.R. 221 (H.L.).

[68]   See ss. 32.1, *ff.,* for further exemptions.

[69]   See s. 30.6 (CA).

[70]   See s. 32.1(1)(*c*) (CA).

[71]   See s. 32.1(1)(*a*) (CA).

[72]   See s. 32.1(1)(*b*) (CA).

[73]   See s. 32.1(1)(*d*), (2) and (3) (CA).

[74]   See s. 30.7 (CA).

(d) the reproduction of a work at the request of a person with a perceptual disability into a format designed for such persons.[75]

5. Enforcement Action

The full range of remedies are available for an infringement of copyright in a work.[76] As in the case of certain types of copyright infringing conduct, there are summary remedies providing quasi-criminal penalties for certain infringements of copyright.[77]

Canadian copyright law now provides that a plaintiff can recover statutory damages for certain infringements.[78] The statutory damages will be between $500 to $20,000 with provisions to permit the courts to reduce the statutory damages where a single work is involved and the amount would be grossly out of proportion to the infringement. The courts can also award punitive damages in an appropriate case. The law also provides that a collective society may elect to recover between three to ten times the statutory licence fees set by the Copyright Board.

6. Types of Things Protected

A literary, musical, dramatic or artistic work, whether or not still subject to any copyright protection, may be the subject of copyright claims by the copyright owner. More specific detail of performers' rights, broadcasters' rights and rights of owners in sound recordings is provided in Chapter 4, "Neighbouring Rights".

(a) Literary Works

Literary works encompass many forms of new technology as well as such traditional types of works as writings. Literary works are defined in s. 2 of the

---

[75] See s. 32 (CA).

[76] See s. 34(1.01) (CA), which provides remedies by way of injunction, damages or accounts and otherwise are available to the owner of the copyright. In addition see s. 34(1) (CA), which provides for clarification of the rights for delivery. Section 35 provides that a plaintiff cannot recover double damages and s. 38(5) addresses claims for damages for conversion or possession of infringing copies or plates.

[77] See s. 42(1) (CA), providing, for example, that the knowing sale or rental of any infringing work, or infringing reproduction of a work, or wide spread distribution of a work is a hybrid offence making the defendant liable on summary conviction for a maximum fine of $25,000 or imprisonment of six months or both, or on indictment a maximum fine of $1,000,000 or imprisonment of five years or both. [Note: this issue formerly dealt with in s. 43.1(1).]

[78] See s. 38.1 (CA). [Note: not yet in force at time of printing.]

Copyright Act to include tables, computer programs[79] and compilations of literary works (*i.e.*, encyclopaedia or databases).[80]

Other examples include books,[81] written instructions, business letters,[82] poems, text of brochures, text portion of a game, lyrics of a song (without music)[83] or contracts.[84] Literary works have been expansively interpreted to include computer programs stored on semi-conductor chips, directories, encoded messages, racing schedules or programs,[85] standard forms,[86] and tables of numbers or other data. In *Bulman Group Ltd. v. "One Write" Accounting Systems Ltd.*,[87] the Court interpreted a literary work to have the requirement only of "functionally assisting, guiding, or pointing the way to some end".

There is no requirement for a literary work to convey any information.

(b) Dramatic Works

The essence of a dramatic work is the existence of a dramatic element.[88] Dramatic works are defined in s. 2 of the *Copyright Act* to include any piece

---

[79]   See, for example, *Apple Computer Inc. v. Mackintosh Computers Ltd.* (1986), 10 C.P.R. (3d) 1, 8 C.I.P.R. 153, 28 D.L.R. (4th) 178 (Fed. T.D.), vard (1987), 16 C.I.P.R. 15 (Fed. C.A.), affd (1990), 71 D.L.R. (4th) 95, 30 C.P.R. (3d) 257 (S.C.C.), which provides an extensive examination of the protection available for computer programs in human readable and machine readable forms, including firmware stored on a semi-conductor chip.

[80]   Examples of compilations or databases enjoying copyright protection include examinations, see *University of London Press Ltd. v. University Tutorial Press Ltd.*, [1916] 2 Ch. 601 (U.K.); and listings of sporting events, see *Football League Ltd. v. Littlewoods Pools Ltd.*, [1959] 1 Ch. 637, [1959] 2 All E.R. 546 (U.K.); *Ascot Jockey Club Ltd. v. Simons* (1968), 64 W.W.R. 411 (B.C. S.C.); or *Ladbroke (Football) Ltd. v. William Hill (Football) Ltd.*, [1964] 1 All E.R. 465 (H.L.). See, however, *Tele-Direct (Publications) Inc. v. American Business Information Inc.* (1996), 74 C.P.R. (3d) 72 (Fed. T.D.) which found little copyright subject-matter in a telephone directory.

[81]   See, for example, *Pasickniak v. Dojacek*, [1928] 2 D.L.R. 545 (Man. C.A.).

[82]   See, for example, *British Oxygen Co. v. Liquid Air Ltd.*, [1925] 1 Ch. 383 (U.K.).

[83]   See, for example, *Ludlow Music Inc. v. Canint Music Corp.*, [1967] 2 Ex. C.R. 109, 51 C.P.R. 278, 62 D.L.R. (2d) 200, 35 Fox Pat. C. 114 (Ex. Ct.).

[84]   See, for example, *Arcon Canada Inc. v. Arcobec Aluminium Inc.* (1984), 7 C.P.R. (3d) 382 (Que. S.C.).

[85]   See, for example, *Ascot Jockey Club Ltd. v. Simons* (1968), 64 W.W.R. 411 (B.C. S.C.); or *Ladbroke (Football) Ltd. v. William Hill (Football) Ltd.*, [1964] 1 All E.R. 465 (H.L.).

[86]   See, for example, *Bulman Group Ltd. v. Alpha One–Write Systems British Columbia Ltd.* (1981), 54 C.P.R. (2d) 179 (Fed. C.A.), revg (1981), 54 C.P.R. (2d) 171 (Fed. T.D.).

[87]   (1982), 62 C.P.R. (2d) 149 (Fed. T.D.).

[88]   For example, a professional sporting event in which the outcome is not known and in which no producer controls the scenic arrangements and action is not a dramatic work: see *Canadian Admiral Corp. v. Rediffusion Inc.*, [1954] Ex. C.R. 382 (Ex. Ct.).

for recitation, choreographic work or mime, the scenic arrangement or acting form of which is fixed in writing or otherwise, any cinematograph and any compilation of dramatic works.

Examples of dramatic works might include radio plays,[89] television or film scripts,[90] screenplays, commercials, training films or videos, movies or in certain cases, films or video-based productions. What is important in characterizing the work as a dramatic work is not the storage media (*i.e.*, compact disk ("CD"), digital versatile disk ("DVD"), video, film, CD-ROM, etc.) but the existence of the dramatic element in the work.

A dramatic work requires a scenic arrangement or acting form (*i.e.*, the dramatic element). As a result, a movie or telecast of a live football game was unable to claim copyright protection.[91] If a producer has arranged the events, then the production may be a dramatic work such as, for example, a radio sketch[92] or an instructional set of video cassettes.

Choreographic work is defined to include any work of choreography, whether or not it has any story line. Cinematograph is defined to include any work produced by any process analogous to cinematography.

If an audio-visual based work is not a dramatic work then it may still qualify as an artistic work.

(c) Musical Works

Musical works require a musical composition. Musical works are defined in s. 2 of the *Copyright Act* to mean any work of music or musical composition, with or without words, and includes any compilation thereof. As a result a collection of songs is also protected as a musical work. A musical work requires either words and music or music alone. Lyrics (the text of a song) alone, like a poem, may be a literary work.

A song including extracts sampled from other works may be a musical work (although any copyright or other issues arising from the use of the other works must be addressed). Under Canadian law the lyrics and music of a song have been held to comprise a single musical work.[93]

---

[89] See, for example, *Kantel v. Grant*, [1933] Ex. C.R. 84 (Ex. Ct.).

[90] See, for example, *Hutton v. C.B.C.* (1989), 27 C.I.P.R. 12, 29 C.P.R. (3d) 398 (Alta. Q.B.).

[91] See, for example, *Canadian Admiral Corp. v. Rediffusion Inc.*, [1954] Ex. C.R. 382 (Ex. Ct.).

[92] See, for example, *Kantel v. Grant*, [1933] Ex. C.R. 84 (Ex. Ct.): author of a radio sketch was able to assert a claim of copyright in that sketch when another person took over the series.

[93] See *Ludlow Music Inc. v. Canint Music Corp.*, [1967] 2 Ex C.R. 109, 51 C.P.R. 278, 62 D.L.R. (2d) 200, 35 Fox Pat. C. 114 (Ex. Ct.).

(d) Artistic Works

Artistic works are a broadly growing category that require some form of visual representation. Section 2 of the *Copyright Act* defines artistic works to include paintings, drawings, maps, charts, plans, photographs, engravings, sculptures, works of artistic craftsmanship, architectural works and compilations of artistic works. Architectural work is defined in s. 2 to mean any building or structure or any model of a building or structure and includes building plans.[94]

Examples of artistic works might include engineering plans,[95] flow charts, schematic diagrams, graphic layouts for brochures or product packaging, some product designs,[96] logos[97] and in certain cases DVD, film, video, laser disk or CD ROM-based works. If there is a dramatic element present such latter works may be dramatic works.

Artistic works recognize two sub-categories of engravings[98] and photographs.[99] Engravings are further defined in s. 2 to include etchings, lithographs, woodcuts, prints and other similar works, not being photographs. Photograph is further defined in s. 2 to include "photo-lithograph and any work expressed by any process analogous to photography".

Motion picture films qualify as a series of connected photographs. Television-based productions stored on DVD, video tape, laser disk or CD-ROM or otherwise do not appear to qualify as photographs. They may be dramatic works depending on the content or artistic works.

It had been suggested that the layout screens to make semi-conductor chips may qualify as photographs or engravings depending on the mode of

---

[94]   See, for example, *Hay v. Sloan* (1957), 27 C.P.R. 132 (Ont. H.C.); *Lifestyle Homes Ltd. v. Randall Homes Ltd.* (1990), 30 C.P.R. (3d) 76 (Man. Q.B.), affd (1991), 34 C.P.R. (3d) 505 (Man. C.A.): copyright in building plans.

[95]   See, for example, *C.P. Koch Ltd. v. Continental Steel Ltd.* (1984), 82 C.P.R. (2d) 156 (B.C. S.C.), affd (1985), 4 C.P.R. (3d) 395 (B.C. C.A.).

[96]   See, for example, *Cuisenaire v. South West Imports Ltd.*, [1969] S.C.R. 208; *George Hensher Ltd. v. Restawile Upholstery (Lancs.) Ltd.*, [1974] 2 All E.R. 420 (H.L.). See also Chapter 6, "Industrial Design" regarding the limits of copyright protection for designs of useful articles.

[97]   See, for example, *DRG Inc. v. Datafile Ltd.*, [1988] 2 F.C. 243 (T.D.), affd (1991), 117 N.R. 308 (Fed. C.A.); *Motel 6 Inc. v. No. 6 Motel Ltd.* (1981), 56 C.P.R. (2d) 44, 127 D.L.R. (3d) 267, [1982] 1 F.C. 638 (T.D.).

[98]   See, for example, *Charles Walker & Co. Ltd. v. The British Picker Co. Ltd.*, [1967] 3 R.P.C. 57; *Martin v. Polyplas Manufacturers Ltd.*, [1969] N.Z.L.R. 1046 (N.Z.S.C.).

[99]   See, for example, *Bauman v. Fussell*, [1978] 14 R.P.C. 487 (C.A.); *Fetherling v. Boughner* (1978), 40 C.P.R. (2d) 253 (Ont. H.C.).

manufacture but any possibility of such copyright protection has been excluded by statute.[100]

(e) Sound Recordings/Mechanical Contrivances

In addition to protection of music works, there is a separate category of works protected by copyright commonly known as mechanical contrivances. In modern copyright law this category of works includes sound recordings.

One of the sole rights of the copyright holder is the right in the case of a literary, dramatic or musical work, to make any sound recording, cinematographic film or other contrivance by means of which the work may be mechanically performed or delivered.[101] Soundtracks of movies are excluded. The maker of a sound recording has a copyright in that recording. That right gives the maker the sole right to reproduce, publish or rent the sound recording.

Examples of contrivances might include DVD, records, cassette or other tapes, compact disks, CD-ROMs, laser disks, semi-conductor chips or other methods used to store and then "mechanically" reproduce sounds.

(f) Communications Signal

Broadcasters and others may acquire rights in a "communications signal".[102] This work is defined to mean radio frequency waves transmitted without the aid of an artificial waveguide and is intended for reception by the public. This new work arises from the broadcast of a communications signal.

So long as the broadcaster has its headquarters in Canada or a World Trade Organization ("WTO") or Rome Convention country and the broadcast originates from that country, the broadcaster has the sole right to fix the communications signal, reproduce the communications signal, perform a television communication signal in a place available to the public on payment of an entrance fee or authorize simultaneous retransmission of the communications signal.

---

[100] Subsection 64.2(1) (CA), precludes copyright protection for such layouts. See Chapter 5, "Integrated Circuit Topographies".

[101] Paragraph 3(1)(*d*) (CA).

[102] See s. 21 (CA).

7. Formal Requirements for Protection

There are limited formal requirements which, once met, result in automatic creation of copyright. The copyright in a work may be registered and such registration may lead to useful presumptions.[103]

Certain formal conditions must be satisfied in order to come within the protection of the *Copyright Act*. Briefly these are:

(a) Characteristics of the Author

The author must be, at the date of creation of the work:

(a) a British subject; or

(b) a citizen or subject of, or a person ordinarily resident in a Berne Convention country; or

(c) a resident within Her Majesty's Realms and Territories; or

(d) a citizen or subject of a Country to which the Minister has extended protection by notice in the *Canada Gazette*.

(b) Character of the Work

The work must come within the class of protected works protected under s. 5(1): "copyright shall subsist . . . in every original literary, dramatic, musical and artistic work". The requirements of originality, fixation and the features which make up literary, musical, artistic and dramatic works and mechanical contrivances are described below.

(i) Original Work

"Original" is defined in a negative sense, meaning essentially that the work is not copied from someone else's work.[104] To be original, the work must emanate from the author. It must be the product of the author's labour and skill and an expression of his or her thoughts and creativity. Copyright is only concerned with the form of expression and so it is this form which must be original. The ideas underlying the form of expression need not be original.[105]

---

[103] See *Protection of Copyright and Industrial Design, supra*, footnote 47, for more details of the process for registration of copyright. Important rebuttable presumptions include that copyright subsists in the work and that the person named is the owner.

[104] See *Canadian Admiral Corp. v. Rediffusion Inc.*, [1954] Ex. C.R. 382 (Ex. Ct.).

[105] The valuable part of a formula, product design or a business concept may often lie not in its form of expression, but rather in the ideas that underlie that form. This is *not* protected by copyright law. It may, however, be protected under trade secret law by imposing

(ii) *Requirement of Fixation*

The work, to be capable of copyright protection, must be fixed in a tangible form.[106] Through the requirement of fixation, the work has some form of permanence. Fixation provides a tangible work against which an alleged copy can be contrasted. The requirement of fixation is an indication of the difficulty the law has in dealing with transient or intangible phenomenon.

In a dramatic work, "the scenic arrangement or acting form must be fixed in writing or otherwise".[107] Computer programs must be "expressed, fixed, embodied or stored in any manner". The requirement of fixation is generally satisfied in the case of computer programs, since they will be "fixed" in some form of magnetic, optical or other medium.

8. Term of Protection

The term of copyright is very long. Copyright protection always ends on December 31 of the last year of protection. The general rule (for most works or situations) is that copyright will subsist for the life of the author plus the end of the year in which the author dies plus fifty years.[108] In the case of joint authors, the term of copyright in the work is the life of the author who dies last plus the end of the year in which they die plus fifty years.[109]

Since the term of copyright is so long one may encounter situations where one wishes to reproduce (or otherwise use) certain materials. In many cases the author of the materials may not be known. If the identity of the author is unknown, the term of copyright in the work will be the earlier of either:

(a) the end of the year of first publication of the work anywhere plus fifty years; or

(b) the end of the year of the making of the work plus seventy-five years.[110]

In the case of unpublished literary, dramatic, musical works or engravings the term of copyright will be the end of the year of first

---

obligations of confidence on users of the business concept or formulae or other confidential information. See Chapter 11, "Trade Secrets".

[106] See, for example, *Canadian Admiral Corp. v. Rediffusion Inc.*, *supra*, footnote 104, finding that a live telecast of a professional football game was not capable of copyright protection because, among other reasons, it was not fixed prior to broadcast.

[107] For example, see *Kantel v. Grant*, [1933] Ex. C.R. 84 (Ex. Ct.), where a radio sketch outline, recorded in writing, was found to be a protectable work.

[108] See s. 6 (CA).

[109] See s. 9(1) (CA).

[110] See s. 6.1 (CA).

publication or public performance plus fifty years.[111] Modern provisions provide that where a work has not been published, performed in public or communicated to the public before the author's death and after the coming into force of S.C. 1997, c. 24, then the copyright will subsist until the end of the year in which the provision comes into force and fifty years thereafter whether or not it is published or otherwise made available to the public. Where the author died more than 100 years before the provision comes into force then the copyright in the work shall subsist until the end of the year in which the provision comes into force and five years thereafter whether or not it is published or otherwise made available to the public.

Copyright in photographs formerly subsisted for the end of the year of the making of the negative, plate or photograph plus fifty years[112] but now can have a hybrid term of the end of the year plus fifty years for corporate owner and the term of protection of the life of the author plus the end of the year in which the author dies plus fifty years for non-corporate owners or when a person owns the majority of the shares of the corporation and that person would otherwise have been qualified as the author.[113]

Copyright in sound recordings or other contrivances by means of which sounds may be mechanically reproduced subsists for the end of the year of the fixing of the sound recording plus fifty years.[114]

Copyright in cinematographs subsists for the end of the year of the first publishing of the cinematograph or if not published within fifty years, for the end of that year plus fifty years.[115]

Copyright in works prepared for Her Majesty or any government department and in which Her Majesty owns copyright subsists for the end of the year of the first publication of the work plus fifty years.[116]

If the author is the first owner of the copyright, the author *cannot* assign copyright to another person (except by will) until twenty-five years after the death of the author. That portion of the copyright revests in the author's estate.[117] A compulsory licence was formerly available to permit reproduction of a work twenty-five years after the death of the author in certain cases.[118]

---

[111]   See s. 7 (CA). Theoretically, the copyright in such an unpublished or unperformed work may exist forever. The amendment to this section by S.C. 1997, c. 24, s. 6, reduced this term.

[112]   See s. 10(1) (CA).

[113]   See s. 10 (CA). [Note, this issue formerly dealt with in s. 6.]

[114]   See s. 23(1)(*b*) (CA). [Note, this issue formerly dealt with in s. 11.]

[115]   See s. 11.1 (CA).

[116]   See s. 12 (CA).

[117]   See s. 14(1) (CA).

[118]   See s. 8(1) (CA).

9. Ownership of the Rights

Conflicts regarding ownership of copyright are one of the basic problems which arise from a system of automatic creation of rights. In many cases the author owns the copyright. The rights arise automatically on creation of the applicable work.

The basic principle provides that copyright will reside with the author of the work.[119] Where the author is an employee and creates a work within the scope of his employment, then the employer is entitled to the copyright.[120] The exception to the general rule only applies if

(a) the author is in a true master-servant relationship; and

(b) the work is created within the scope of that relationship.

For example, where a graphic designer is a consultant, and in the absence of any agreement to the contrary, the graphic designer will own the copyright in a logo or art work prepared for the customer.[121] The same is true for other works, such as computer programs or engineering reports or plans, created by independent contractors.[122]

There are further, specialized rules which relate to more specific situations. These are described below.

Where an engraving, photograph or portrait is ordered by a person and is made for valuable consideration, unless there is an agreement to the contrary, the commissioner will own the copyright.[123]

Works prepared under the direction and control of Her Majesty or any government department, unless there is an agreement to the contrary, Her Majesty will own the copyright in the work.[124]

The owner of copyright in photographs is the person who either

---

[119] See s. 13(1) (CA). See, for example, *Commercial Signs v. General Motors Products of Canada Ltd.*, [1937] 2 D.L.R. 310 (Ont. H.C.), affd [1937] 2 D.L.R. 800 (Ont. C.A.); *Benjamin Distribution Ltd. v. Éditions Flammarion Ltée* (1982), 68 C.P.R. (2d) 251 (Que. C.A.).

[120] See s. 13(3) (CA).

[121] Provided it does not fall within the commissioned works exemption. See s. 13(2) (CA).

[122] See, for example, *University of London Press Ltd. v. University Tutorial Press Ltd.*, [1916] 2 Ch. 601 (U.K.): copyright in examinations; *Silverson v. Neon Products Ltd.* (1978), 39 C.P.R. (2d) 234 (B.C. S.C.): copyright in a sign design; *Northern Office Micro Computers v. Rosenstein* (1981), (4) S.A. 123, [1982] F.S.R. 124 (S.C.S.A.): copyright in computer programs.

[123] See s. 13(2) (CA).

[124] See s. 12 (CA).

(a) was the owner of the original negative or other plate at the time the negative or plate was made, or

(b) was the owner of the original photograph at the time it was made if there was no negative or other plate (*i.e.*, an instant or digital photograph where no negative is involved in the process of making the photograph).[125]

The owner of copyright in a sound recording or other mechanical contrivance by means of which sounds may be mechanically reproduced is the maker, the person responsible for making the arrangements necessary for first fixation of the sounds.[126]

In certain types of works an author may consciously or unconsciously draw from a number of sources in completing the work. This may raise the risk of infringement. It is also possible that there may be a number of different authors who contributed different portions to the work and hence also have certain ownership claims.

Note that the industrial design ownership rules are different.[127] Note, also, that authors own moral rights and performers may own performers' rights which may be separate from the copyright in the work which is created or performed.[128]

Copyrights, unlike moral rights, may be assigned by the author.[129] Assignments of copyright must comply with certain formalities – the assignment must be in writing and filed at the copyright office.[130]

10. Special Rules

(a) Registration

In Canada, copyright arises without formality and so there is no formal requirement for registration or notification in order for a copyright to subsist in an appropriate work.[131] There is a register for copyrights in Canada, but its

---

[125]   See s. 10(2) (CA).

[126]   See s. 18 (CA).

[127]   This may result in different owners of copyright and industrial design rights in the same work or design. See Chapter 6, "Industrial Design".

[128]   See Chapter 3 for more information on Moral Rights and Chapter 4 for more information on Performers' Rights.

[129]   See s. 13(4) (CA).

[130]   See s. 13(4) (CA).

[131]   As discussed above, the principle of automatic copyright protection without formalities is a feature of the Berne Convention, an international copyright treaty, to which Canada is a party. It is discussed in Chapter 14.

value is evidentiary in nature. Registration provides certain useful presumptions which would assist in an action enforcing the right.[132] The Supreme Court of Canada in *Circle Film Enterprises Inc. v. C.B.C.*[133] held that registration may give rise to a rebuttable presumption of copyright.[134]

There are a number of legal advantages to registration of copyright, particularly in enforcement of the copyright against infringers. The registration of a copyright or of a licence or assignment acts as constructive notice of the applicable rights. This may be important if the assignor or licensor purported to grant the same rights to another person.[135] Registration would act as constructive notice to negative any assumption of innocent copying. This provides a means to claim statutory damages available under S.C. 1997, c. 24.

(b) Notice

No notice is required to create enforceable copyright in Canada. While no notice is required, use of a notice may enhance domestic and international protection of the work. A form of copyright notice useful to seek certain international protection as well as to take advantage of the presumptions under the *Copyright Act* is described below. The placement of a notice may create presumptions which may assist in litigation.[136]

The principle of automatic copyright protection without formalities is a feature of the Berne Convention, an international copyright treaty, to which Canada is a party (see Chapter 14). The Universal Copyright Convention ("UCC"), another international treaty, provides a basis for international recognition of copyright. Under the UCC a form of copyright notice is a condition precedent to a claim of rights under that treaty. That form of notice is discussed below. It is common to see copyright notices in works emanating from American authors since the United States was historically based on a registry and notice system of copyright.

Compliance with the UCC is also a means to seek to establish a clear claim for copyright protection in the United States under the domestic law.

---

[132]   See s. 34(3) (CA).

[133]   [1959] S.C.R. 602.

[134]   In *Blue Crest Music Inc. v. Canusa Records Inc.* (1974), 17 C.P.R. (2d) 149 (Fed. T.D.), it was held that where copyright is presumed to exist, then originality is also presumed.

[135]   Subsection 13(4) (CA) has been held to require that any assignment or licence of copyright should be registered in order to be the basis of enforceable rights against third parties. See *Motel 6 Inc. v. No. 6 Motel Ltd.* (1981), 127 D.L.R. (3d) 267 (Fed. T.D.). Quaere whether a court would consider any change in this law by the re-enactment of s. 13(4) by 1997, c. 24.

[136]   See s. 34(4) (CA).

The UCC stipulates that the following form of copyright notice is mandatory and must be prominently displayed on a work:

© year of publication   name of owner

An example of the notice is:

© 1998 Martin Kratz.

The © symbol is specifically mandated by the UCC. The year is the year of first publication of the work. The name is the identity of the copyright owner. This form of copyright notice is also recognized as a proper notice under the domestic copyright law of the United States.[137]

Copyright owners may supplement the copyright notice with other terms. Many publishers add extensive prohibitions on reproduction of the book. While the UCC notice is intended for published works, some try to use it for unpublished works as well. Often the unpublished works may contain confidential information the owner wishes to protect.

(c) Overlapping Rights

It has been suggested that copyright does not extend to drawings in patent specifications.[138] Copyright co-exists with trade secret law and provides very useful rights to complement the rights obtained under a trademark registration.

Copyright and trademark rights may co-exist in a logo. Unlike a trademark which only provides protection in relation to specific uses, copyright provides protection in relation to any substantially similar copy regardless of use.

---

[137]   Another element one may use under American copyright law if the © symbol can not be used is: "Copyright". Many publishers use both, as follows: Copyright © , together with the year and owner information.

[138]   See *Rucker Co. v. Gavel's Vulcanizing Ltd.* (1985), 6 C.I.P.R. 137 (Fed. T.D.), vard (1987), 14 C.P.R. (3d) 439 (Fed. T.D.).

3

Moral Rights

1. Introduction

In many cases an author's work may be an expression of the author's personality and an extension of the author's ego and sense of self. Mutilation of the work or use other than as contemplated by the author may impact on the author's reputation. In order to protect some of these personal rights the *Copyright Act* provides for specific moral rights of the author.

Until June 6, 1988 the author had quite limited moral rights in Canada.[1] Since the law reforms introduced on June 7, 1988, a more substantial code of moral rights have been provided and continue to develop.

The moral rights give the author a degree of control over subsequent use or dealings with a work even in cases where the author has sold the work to another or, further, even where the author has assigned copyright in the work to another.

2. Scope of Rights

The moral rights may be described as

(a) a paternity right;

(b) an integrity right; and

(c) an association right.

The specific rights are described below.

(a) Paternity Right

The author has the right to assert paternity of the work or require the author's name to be associated with the work if reasonable in the circumstances. Further, where reasonable in the circumstances, the author has

---

[1]   See s. 12.7 (CA), prior to the 1988 reforms.

the right to be associated with the work under a pseudonym or the right to remain anonymous.[2] Note that this right (as do other moral rights) applies even if the author is not the owner of the copyright in the work. As a result an employee working in the scope of employment in making a work will retain this paternity right (and other moral rights) even though the employer owns the copyright in the work. Thus, unless these rights are waived, the employee can insist on being identified as the author and, where reasonable in the circumstances, be associated with the work.

(b) Integrity Right

The author has the right to object to or restrain certain uses of or dealings with a work if the use or dealing is to the prejudice of the honour or reputation of the author.[3] The acts the author may complain of are if the work is distorted, mutilated or otherwise modified. For example, a mall owner hanging Christmas ornaments on a sculpture was found to have violated the moral rights of the sculptor even though the mall owner owned the sculpture.[4] It has also been suggested that the modification of a computer program and its graphic display may infringe this right.[5] In many cases there may be an implied right to modify the work, such as in the case of engineering drawings or plans.[6]

Disputes between authors and editors may give rise to integrity claims. Editors must often modify a work to meet the needs of the market or publishing format. Authors may be offended by changes made to their words. For example, where an editor substantially revised an article making numerous errors of fact and altered the title, style and the conclusion of the article the Court found the editor had a right to shorten the article, that style is a matter of taste but that the author is not bound to have his or her name associated with an article expressing other opinions in another's style.[7]

The prejudice to the author's honour or reputation is deemed to have occurred with any distortion, mutilation or other modification of a sculpture,

---

[2]   See s. 14.1 (CA).

[3]   See s. 28.2 (CA).

[4]   *Snow v. Eaton Centre Ltd.* (1982), 70 C.P.R. (2d) 105 (Ont. H.C.).

[5]   See *Nintendo of America Inc. v. Camerica Corp.* (1991), 34 C.P.R. (3d) 193 (Fed. T.D.), affd (1991), 36 C.P.R. (3d) 352 (Fed. C.A.).

[6]   See *Netupsky v. Dominion Bridge Co.* (1971), 3 C.P.R. (2d) 1 (S.C.C.).

[7]   Publishing contracts typically provide for such a right.

painting or engraving.[8] As a result no proof of damage to the author's honour or reputation is necessary in respect of such works.[9]

(c) Association Right

The author has the right to object to or restrain any use of a work in association with a product, service, cause or institution where such conduct would be to the prejudice of the honour and reputation of the author.[10] For example, use of a design or style of art for which an author is well-known in association with a disreputable business may damage the reputation of the author of the design.[11]

3. Enforcement of Moral Rights

The full range of remedies are available for an infringement of moral rights in a work.[12] Similarly some conduct may claim the protection of statutory defences to both copyright infringement actions and moral rights infringement actions.[13]

Limitations on enforcement of moral rights include the requirement to bring action within three years of the cause of action.[14]

Merely changing the location of a work or the physical means by which a work is exposed or the physical structure containing a work is not, by that act alone, a distortion, mutilation or other modification of the work.[15] Similarly steps taken in good faith to restore or preserve a work are not, by that act alone, a distortion, mutilation or other modification of the work.[16]

---

[8]   See s. 28.2(2) (CA).

[9]   Some art collectors may fear that these rights are subjectively determined and may be exercised to limit the collector's enjoyment of the work. This has led to a common practice by many collectors of such works of art in seeking blanket waivers of moral rights from authors of such works.

[10]   See s. 28.2(1)(*b*) (CA).

[11]   This moral right should be considered in the creation of works intended to be used for a commercial purpose. It is suggested that a graphic designer who creates a design trademark (*i.e.*, a logo) or similar work for a customer and for valuable consideration thereby waives this moral right unless the contrary intent is expressed.

[12]   See s. 34(1.1) (CA) which provides remedies by way of injunction, damages, accounts or delivery up and otherwise are available to the moral rights claimant.

[13]   See, for example, s. 64.1(1) (CA), which provides that application of useful features of a utilitarian article is not an infringement of either copyright or moral rights in the work or design which is applied to the article.

[14]   See s. 41 (CA).

[15]   See s. 28.2(3)(*a*) (CA).

[16]   See s. 28.2(3)(*b*) (CA).

4. Types of Things Protected

Any work which may be capable of copyright protection may be the subject of moral rights claims by the author.[17] This includes works of traditional artistic content such as paintings, engravings and sculptures but also much less traditional works such as engineering plans[18] and computer programs.[19]

Since moral rights cannot be assigned and since copyright arises in so many situations and in respect of so many types of works, one should always address the moral rights issues, if any, in a work.

5. Formal Requirements for Protection

There are no formal requirements to create moral rights in a work. There must be an author and there must be a work in which copyright subsists. As a result one should consult the formalities required to create copyright in a work.[20]

6. Term of Protection

The moral rights last for the same term as the copyright in the work.[21] As a result the term of the moral right may vary as the term of copyright varies for some types of works.[22] For most works, however, the term of copyright and hence term of moral rights will be the life of the author plus the end of the year in which the author dies plus fifty years.

7. Ownership of the Rights

The author owns the moral rights. The rights arise automatically on creation of the work. Unlike copyrights, the moral rights may not be assigned by the author.[23] Moral rights may, however, be waived.[24]

---

[17]   See Chapter 2, Section 3, "Limits on Copyright", for an indication of the type of things protectable by copyright law.

[18]   *Webb & Knapp (Can.) Ltd. v. Edmonton* (City), [1970] S.C.R. 588.

[19]   *Nintendo of America Inc. v. Camerica Corp.* (1991), 34 C.P.R. (3d) 193 (Fed. T.D.), affd (1991), 36 C.P.R. (3d) 352 (Fed. C.A.).

[20]   See Chapter 2, Section 7, "Formal Requirements for Protection".

[21]   See s. 14.2(1) (CA).

[22]   See Chapter 2, Section 8, "Term of Protection", for details on the term of copyright in different types of works.

[23]   See s. 14.1(2) (CA).

[24]   See s. 14.1(2) (CA).

The waiver of moral rights may be either in whole or in part. Assignment of the copyright in a work does not automatically constitute a waiver of the moral rights in the work.[25] The waiver may be express or implied. To avoid doubt, one should define the scope of any waiver in writing.

The waiver may be limited or unlimited and in either case made in favour of a specific person or unlimited. If the waiver is in favour of either the owner or a licensee of the copyright, it may be invoked by any person authorized by such owner or licensee.[26]

The effect of a waiver of moral rights permits the person for whom the waiver is intended to carry out the conduct which would otherwise be an infringement of the applicable moral rights.

There is a special code identifying rules of succession for moral rights. On the death of the author the moral rights pass to either:

(a) the person to whom they are specifically bequeathed;[27] or

(b) where there is no specific bequest of the moral rights and the author dies testate in respect of the copyright in the work, the person to whom the copyright is bequeathed;[28] or

(c) where there is no person to whom either the moral rights are specifically bequeathed (*i.e.*, situation (a) above) or to whom the copyrights in the work are specifically bequeathed (*i.e.*, situation (b) above) then the person entitled to those moral rights shall be the person entitled to any other property in respect of which the author dies intestate.[29]

As a result it is desirable for each author to specifically bequeath their moral rights to avoid any issues or conflict after death.

8. Special Rules

Collectors of artistic works should note that the author (artist) has not only moral rights but also a display right — that is a sole right to present at a public exhibition, for a purpose other than sale or hire, an artistic work made after June 7, 1988 or to authorize another to do so.[30] This display right is part of the copyright in the work. Unlike the moral rights, the display right may be assigned and like the moral rights the display right can be the subject of a licence or waiver. This display right does not apply to maps, charts or plans.

---

[25]   See s. 14.1(3) (CA).

[26]   See s. 14.1(4) (CA).

[27]   See s. 14.2(2)(*a*) (CA).

[28]   See s. 14.2(2)(*b*) (CA).

[29]   See s. 14.2(2)(*c*) (CA).

[30]   See s. 3(1)(*g*) (CA).

Many collectors may seek to donate a work they had purchased to a public gallery or museum or may wish to sell the work to others. If the purchaser wishes to display the work in public (*e.g.*, in the public entrance or waiting area of a business) then the right to display the work in public may be required. As a result such collectors should consider obtaining both applicable waivers of moral rights and at least a licence to display the work in public.

In many cases it may be important that the owner of copyright in a work which is intended to be used for a commercial purpose obtain a partial or complete waiver of these moral rights so as to ensure the owner has unfettered use of the work. Obtaining a waiver of moral rights should be considered in any case where:

(a) the true author may not be named; or

(b) there may be subsequent modifications or adjustments may need to be made to a work or design; or

(c) where the work (*i.e.*, a design mark) may be used in association with a product, business, cause or institution.

4

Neighbouring Rights

1. Introduction

Neighbouring rights are certain rights related to the existence or creation of copyright in a work. These rights provide regulation of a variety of industries that are largely based on use of copyright materials. Neighbouring rights consist of performers' rights, broadcasters' rights and rights of makers of sound recordings and related provisions. Many of the copyright provisions seen in Chapter 2 may also be applicable to such neighbouring rights.

Intellectual property law does not universally recognize nor protect all forms of creativity.[1] In many countries performers were able to protect certain aspects of their performances under so-called performers' rights. The interpretation a performer may give to a copyright protected work (*e.g.*, a musical or dramatic work) may itself be a reflection of considerable creative expression.

Performers' rights give the author a degree of control over subsequent use or dealings with the acoustic or visual representation of a dramatic work and the performer's performance of the work. The other neighbouring rights give broadcasters and makers of sound recordings rights important in controlling certain subject-matter used in their applicable industry.

A key feature of performers' rights is a pre-existing work. This pre-existing work may, depending on the circumstances, be literary, artistic, dramatic or musical. Further, the performer may acquire rights in a performance of the pre-existing work even if the pre-existing work is no longer the subject of copyright protection.

---

[1] A good example of a substantial field of creative expression not well-protected by intellectual property law is that of useful works or designs. If the designs do not appeal to the eye, industrial design protection is not available. Protection of useful features are excluded by s. 64.1(1) (CA) and s. 5.1 of the *Industrial Design Act*, R.S.C. 1985, c. 10 (4th Supp.), s. 21. If the design does not meet the high standard of an invention, little protection is available to the designer.

After conclusion of the Uruguay round of the General Agreement on Tariffs and Trade (GATT), Canada agreed to provide for protection of performers' rights.[2] These rights were enacted by amendments to the *Copyright Act* which came into force on January 1, 1996.[3] In addition, included in phase two of copyright reform, Canada subsequently introduced expanded performers' and other neighbouring rights.[4]

These recent legislative provisions replaced the earlier performers rights and expanded the neighbouring rights to include broadcasters' rights, rights of makers of sound recordings and other provisions necessary for Canada to join the Rome Convention.[5]

2. Scope of Rights — Performers' Rights

Performers' rights may be described as the following rights:

(a) a fixation right;

(b) a reproduction right;

(c) a communication right;

(d) a performance right; and

(e) a rental right.

These rights are described below.

(a) Fixation Right

The fixation right has the greatest application to musical works. If the performer's performance has not been fixed, the owner of the performers' right has the sole right to fix the performer's performance, or any substantial part thereof, by means of a sound recording by means of which sounds may be mechanically reproduced.[6]

A "performer's performance" means

---

[2]   For more details see Chapter 14, "International Treaties". See also Final Act Embodying the Results of the Uruguay Round of Multilateral Trade Negotiations, done at Marrakech, Morocco, April 15, 1994, Annex 1C: Agreement on Trade-Related Aspects of Intellectual Property Rights, April 15, 1994.

[3]   See *An Act to Amend the Copyright Act*, S.C. 1994, c. 47.

[4]   *Ibid.*

[5]   Formally known as The Convention for the Protection of Performers, Producers or Phonograms and Broadcasting Organizations (1961). See s. 91 (CA). See also S.C. 1997, c. 24, s. 56, which preserves rights which arise under the former s. 14.01 of the *Copyright Act*.

[6]   See s. 15(1)(*a*)(iii) (CA). The concept of record, perforated roll or other contrivance is replaced with sound recordings.

(a) a performance[7] of an artistic work, dramatic work or musical work,[8] whether or not the work was previously fixed in any material form, and whether or not the work's term of copyright protection under the *Copyright Act* has expired,[9]

(b) a recitation or reading[10] of a literary work,[11] whether or not the work's term of copyright protection under the *Copyright Act* has expired,[12] or

(c) an improvisation[13] of a dramatic work, musical work or literary work, whether or not the improvised work is based on a pre-existing work.[14]

The 1997 amendments expanded the definition of performance to include any acoustic or visual representation of

(a) the performer's performance,

(b) sound recording, and

(c) a communications signal.

(b) Reproduction Right

If the performer's performance is fixed, the owner of the performers' right has the sole right to reproduce an unauthorized fixation.[15] If authorized, the owner has the right to reproduce the fixation or any substantial part thereof and any reproduction of that fixation, or any substantial part of that reproduction so long as such fixation was made for a purpose other than that for which the consent of the owner of the performers' right.[16] If not authorized the owner has the right to reproduce that unauthorized fixation.[17] This provision gives the owner of the performers' right a degree of control over unauthorized copies of, for example, a compact disk ("CD"), digital video

---

[7]   Before the amendments introduced by S.C. 1997, c. 24, the rights were limited to live performances.

[8]   Before the amendments introduced by S.C. 1997, c. 24, rights were limited to pre-existing artistic, musical or dramatic works or a live recitation of a pre-existing literary work.

[9]   Section 2 (CA).

[10]   This was previously limited to live readings.

[11]   Before the 1997 amendments, this was limited to pre-existing literary or dramatic works.

[12]   Section 2 (CA).

[13]   Before the 1997 amendments, rights were limited to live improvisations of artistic, dramatic, musical or literary works.

[14]   Section 2 (CA).

[15]   See s. 15(1)(*b*)(i) (CA).

[16]   See s. 15(1)(*b*)(ii) (CA).

[17]   Section 15(1)(*b*)(i) (CA). [Note: this issue formerly dealt with in s. 14.01(1)(*b*).]

disk ("DVD") or tape which contains the performer's performance of a musical work.

(c) Communication Right

If the performer's performance is not fixed, the owner of the performer's right has the sole right to communicate the performer's performance, or any substantial part thereof, to the public by telecommunication at the time of the performer's performance.[18]

(d) Performance Right

The owner of the performance right has the right to perform the performance in public where it is communicated to the public by telecommunication other than by communication signal.[19]

(e) Rental Right

The owner of the performers' right has the sole right to rent out a sound recording of the performer's performance.[20]

In addition to the sole rights of the performer, the owner of the performers' right also has the right to authorize others to carry out any of the acts contemplated by those sole rights.

It is an infringement of the performers' right in a performer's performance if a person, without the consent of the owner of the performers' right, does any act that only the performer has the right to do.[21]

3. Limits on Performers' Rights

Some substantial defences or limits on performers' rights are:

(a) any fair dealing with the performer's performance, a fixation thereof or a reproduction of the fixation, so long as done for the purposes of private study, research, criticism, review or newspaper summary.[22]

(b) the making of a fixation or reproduction of a performer's performance that is performed live or a sound recording performed at the same time as the performer's performance.[23]

---

[18]   See s. 15(1)(*a*) (CA). See also the provisions of the Act which set out limits on what is a communication to the public by telecommunications.

[19]   See s. 15(1)(*a*)(ii) (CA).

[20]   See s. 15(1)(*c*) (CA).

[21]   See s. 31(1) (CA), formerly s. 28.02 and renumbered by 1997, c. 24, s. 17.

[22]   See ss. 29.1 and 29.2 (CA).

[23]   See s. 30.8 (CA). [Note: not yet in force at time of printing.]

(c) the making of a reproduction of a performer's performance embodied in a sound recording solely to provide it in a format suitable for broadcasting.[24]

(d) if use of a performance is authorized for use in a cinematographic work then the performer may no longer authorize the fixation right, communication right or performance right.[25]

The full range of remedies are available for an infringement of performers' rights in a work.[26] As in the case of certain types of copyright infringing conduct, there are summary remedies providing quasi-criminal penalties for certain infringements of performers' rights.[27]

4. Scope of Rights — Broadcasters' Rights

Broadcasters' rights give broadcasters of communication signals to the public control over some dealings with the communications signal. A "communications signal" means radio frequency waves transmitted to the public without the use of an artificial wave guide (*i.e.*, not using a cable or other such conduit to guide the signal).

Broadcasters' rights may be described as the following sole rights:

(a) a fixation right;

(b) a reproduction right;

(c) retransmission right; and

(d) a communication right.

(a) Fixation Right

The owner of the broadcasters' right has the sole right to fix the communications signal, or any substantial part thereof.[28]

---

[24] See s. 30.9 (CA). [Note: not yet in force at time of printing.]

[25] See s. 17(1) (CA) and the relevant provisions of s. 15(1) (CA).

[26] See s. 34(1.01) (CA), which provides remedies by way of injunction, damages, accounts or delivery up and otherwise are available to the owner of the performers' rights.

[27] See s. 42(1) (CA) [note: this issue formerly dealt with in s. 43.1(1)], providing, for example, that knowing sale or rental of any infringing work, or sale or offer of sale of copyright infringing marks is a hybrid offence making the defendant liable on summary conviction for a maximum fine of $25,000 or imprisonment of six months or both, or on indictment a maximum fine of $1,000,000 or imprisonment of five years or both.

[28] Paragraph 21(1)(*a*) (CA).

(b) Reproduction Right

The owner of the copyright in the communications signal has the sole right to reproduce the fixation (see (a) above)[29] so long as the fixation was made *without* the consent of the owner of the copyright in the communication signal. As an example, this provision gives the owner of the broadcasters' right a degree of control over unauthorized copies of a communications signal containing a musical work.

(c) Retransmission Right

The owner of the copyright in the communications signal has the right to authorize simultaneous retransmission of the communications signal to the public by other broadcasters.[30]

(d) Communication Right

The owner of the copyright in the communications signal has the sole right to perform a television communication signal, or any substantial part thereof, to the public at a place open to the public and to charge an entrance fee therefor.[31]

The 1997 amendments expanded the definition of performance to include any acoustic or visual representation of

(a) a work;

(b) a performer's performance; and

(c) a communications signal or sound recording.[32]

In addition to the sole rights of the broadcaster, the owner of the copyright in the communications signal also has the right to authorize others to carry out any of the acts contemplated by those sole rights.

It is an infringement of the broadcasters' right in a communications signal if a person, without the consent of the owner of the copyright in the communications signal, does any act that only the broadcaster has the right to do.[33]

---

[29]   Paragraph 21(1)(*b*) (CA).

[30]   See s. 21(1)(*c*) (CA).

[31]   See s. 21(1)(*d*) (CA). See also the provisions of the Act defining the extent of communication to the public by telecommunications. For example, persons who occupy apartments, hotel rooms or dwelling units situated in the same building are part of the public and a communication intended to be received exclusively by such persons is a communication to the public. Also if a person's only role is to provide the telecommunication means necessary to communicate the broadcaster's work to the public, that act alone does not communicate the communications signal to the public.

[32]   Section 2 (CA).

[33]   See s. 27 (CA).

5. Limits on Broadcasters' Rights

Some substantial defences or limits on broadcasters' rights are:

(a) any fair dealing with the communications signal, a fixation thereof or a reproduction of the fixation, so long as done for the purposes of private study, research, criticism, review or newspaper summary.[34]

(b) the making of a fixation or reproduction of a communications signal for performance in an educational institution of news and commentary productions (but excluding documentaries).[35]

(c) the making of a fixation or reproduction of a communications signal to comply with any rule under the *Broadcasting Act*, S.C. 1991, c. 11, ss. 1-71.[36]

The full range of remedies are available for an infringement of broadcasters' rights in a communications signal.[37] As in the case of certain types of copyright infringing conduct, there are summary remedies providing quasi-criminal penalties for certain infringements of these rights.[38]

6. Scope of Rights — Makers of Sound Recordings

The maker of a sound recording acquires certain rights in the sound recording. A "sound recording" means a recording made exclusively of sounds and recording in any material form. Soundtracks of a movie are excluded from this definition. The maker of a sound recording is the person who is primarily responsible for the arrangements involved in the recording of sounds.

The rights of makers of sound recordings may be described as the following sole rights:

(a) a publication right;

(b) compensation right for a public performance;

(c) a reproduction right; and

(d) a rental right.

---

[34]   See ss. 29.1 and 29.2 (CA).

[35]   See s. 29.6 (CA). [Note: not yet in force at time of printing.]

[36]   See s. 32.1(1)(*d*) (CA).

[37]   See s. 34(1) (CA).

[38]   See s. 42 (CA).

(a) Publication Right

The owner of the right in the sound recording has the sole right to publish the sound recording, or any substantial part thereof, for the first time by means of a sound recording.[39]

(b) Compensation for a Public Performance

Where the sound recording has been published, the owner of these rights is entitled to equitable compensation for a public performance of the sound recording or a transmission to the public of the sound recording by telecommunication. The 1997 amendments expanded the definition of performance to include any acoustic or visual representation of

(a) the performer's performance;

(b) sound recording; and

(c) a communications signal.

A retransmission of the sound recording to the public gives rise to no additional claim by the owner of that right.[40]

(c) Reproduction Right

The owner of the right in the sound recording has the sole right to reproduce the sound recording or any substantial part thereof in any material form and any reproduction of that fixation, or any substantial part of that reproduction.[41] This provision gives the owner of the right in a sound recording a degree of control over making copies of a DVD, CD or tape which contains a musical work.

(d) Rental Right

The owner of the right in a sound recording has the sole right to rent the sound recording to others.[42]

In addition to the sole rights of the owner of rights in the sound recording, the owner of these rights also has the right to authorize others to carry out any of the acts contemplated by those sole rights.

It is an infringement of the right in a sound recording if a person, without the consent of the owner of that right, does any act that only the owner has the right to do.[43]

---

[39]   Paragraph 18(1)(*a*) (CA).

[40]   See s. 19(1) (CA).

[41]   Paragraph 18(1)(*b*) (CA).

[42]   See s. 18(1)(*c*) (CA).

[43]   See s. 27 (CA).

7.   Limits on Rights of Makers of Sound Recordings

Some substantial defences or limits on rights of makers of sound recordings are:

(a)   any fair dealing with the sound recording, a fixation thereof or a reproduction of the fixation, so long as done for the purposes of private study, research, criticism, review or newspaper summary.[44]

(b)   the making of a performance in public of a sound recording by an educational institution for educational purposes.[45]

(c)   the making of an incidental fixation or reproduction of a sound recording by a programming undertaking in certain circumstances.[46]

(d)   the reproduction of a sound recording into a format more appropriate for broadcasting.[47]

The full range of remedies are available for an infringement of rights of makers of sound recordings in a work.[48]

8.   Types of Things Protected

A literary, musical, dramatic or artistic work, whether or not still subject to any copyright protection, may be the subject of performers' rights.

As noted in Section 2 — "Scope of Rights — Performers' Rights", a "performer's performance" means

(a)   a live performance of a pre-existing artistic work, pre-existing dramatic work or pre-existing musical work, or a live recitation of a pre-existing literary work, whether or not the work was previously fixed in any material form, and whether or not the work's term of copyright protection under the Act has expired,

(b)   a live reading of a pre-existing literary work, dramatic work, whether or not the work's term of copyright protection under the Act has expired, or

(c)   a live improvisation of an artistic work, dramatic work, musical work or literary work, whether or not the improvised work is based on a pre-existing work.[49]

Since a sound recording means a recording made exclusively of sounds in any material form, a sound recording may be a cassette tape, CD, DVD,

---

[44]   See ss. 29.1 and 29.2 (CA).

[45]   See s. 29.5 (CA).

[46]   See ss. 30.8, *ff.* (CA). [Note: not yet in force at time of printing.]

[47]   See ss. 30.9, *ff.* (CA), which limits this right. [Note: not yet in force at time of printing.]

[48]   See s. 34(1) (CA).

[49]   Section 2 (CA).

CD-ROM or may utilize some other media to communicate recorded sounds. Soundtracks of a movie are excluded from this definition. A pre-existing work to be recorded is not necessary.

Since a "communications signal" means radio frequency waves transmitted to the public without the use of an artificial wave guide (*i.e.*, not using a cable or other such conduit to guide the signal), a wide range of works is covered. There need not be a pre-existing work to be communicated by communications signal.

9. Formal Requirements for Protection

(a) Performers' Rights

The formal requirements to create performers' rights in a work are similar to the limited formal requirements for a work to claim protection under copyright law.[50] There must be a performer and there must be a performance. The performer's performance must take place in Canada or a country that is a member of the Rome Convention country and more limited rights exist for performances in WTO member countries.[51] In addition, if the performance is fixed in a sound recording, the sound recording must be fixed by a maker who is a national of Canada or a Rome Convention country. Further, in a case of a sound recording fixing the performance either

(a) the first publication must occur in sufficient numbers to satisfy reasonable demand, or

(b) it must be communicated to the public by a communication signal in either case from such countries.

Note that it is not necessary that copyright subsist in any pre-existing work which is the subject of the performance. The performer may claim certain rights in a live improvisation of an artistic, dramatic, musical or literary work, whether or not the improvised work is based on a pre-existing work.[52]

(b) Communications Signal

The broadcaster of a communications signal must, on making the broadcast, either be a citizen or resident of Canada, a Rome Convention

---

[50]   See ss. 5(1), 15(1), 15(2) (CA) [note: this issue formerly dealt with in s. 14.01(1) providing performers' rights for post-WTO performances. Certain limited rights were provided for performances in countries prior to adherence to the WTO under s. 14.01(4) (CA).]

[51]   See s. 15(2) (CA). See also the more limited right under the former s. 14.01 for performances in WTO countries on or after January 1, 1996.

[52]   Section 2 (CA).

country, or a WTO member country.[53] The first broadcast should occur from that country.

(c) Sound Recordings

The maker of a sound recording must, on fixing the sound recording, be a citizen or resident of Canada, a Rome Convention country, a WTO member country, or a Berne Convention country at first fixation or on first publication.[54] The first publication should occur in sufficient quantities to satisfy reasonable demand in such countries.

10. Term of Protection

(a) Performers' Rights

Performers' rights last for the end of the calender year in which the first performance takes place if not fixed or, if fixed in a sound recording, plus fifty years thereafter.[55]

(b) Communications Signal

The rights in a communications signal last for the end of the calender year in which the communications signal is first broadcast plus fifty years thereafter.[56]

(c) Sound Recordings

The rights in a sound recording last for the end of the calender year in which the sound recording is first fixed plus fifty years thereafter.[57]

11. Ownership of the Rights

(a) Performers' Rights

The performer is the first owner of the performers' rights in the performance. Like copyrights, but unlike moral rights, performers' rights may be assigned by the performer.[58] Assignments of performers' rights must comply with the same types of formalities as required by copyright law.

---

[53]   See s. 21(2) (CA).

[54]   See s. 18(2) (CA).

[55]   See s. 23(1)(*a*) (CA).

[56]   See s. 23(1)(*c*) (CA).

[57]   See s. 23(1)(*b*) (CA).

[58]   See s. 25 (CA), which provides that s. 13(4)-(7) apply to assignments or licences of performers' rights.

It is important to note that an assignment or grant of licence of a performers' right does not affect the ability of the performer to prevent fixation of the performer's performance, or any reproduction of such a fixation, or any substantial part of such a fixation or reproduction where the fixation was made *without* the performer's consent.[59]

An assignment or grant of licence of a performers' right does not affect the ability of the performer to prevent import into Canada, for sale or hire, of any fixation of the performer's performance, or a reproduction of such a fixation, if such a fixation or reproduction was, to the knowledge of the performer, made without the performer's consent. As a result it is desirable for all applicable parties to specifically address their respective interests in any performers' rights to avoid issues or conflict.

(b) Communications Signal

The first owner of the rights in a communications signal is the broadcaster of the communications signal.[60] Like copyrights, the rights in a communications signal may be assigned by the owner.[61] Assignments of such rights must comply with the same types of formalities as required by copyright law.

(c) Sound Recordings

The first owner of the rights in a sound recording is the maker of the sound recording.[62] Like copyrights, the rights in a sound recording may be assigned by the owner.[63] Assignments of such rights must comply with the same types of formalities as required by copyright law.

12. Special Rules

Users of performers' rights particularly in literary, dramatic or musical works should note that there is a right in the copyright holder to make a mechanical contrivance.[64] If such a contrivance is made, there are also rights in the mechanical contrivance itself[65] and in the underlying literary, dramatic

---

[59]   See s. 15(1)(*b*)(i), (ii) (CA).

[60]   See s. 24(*c*) (CA).

[61]   See s. 25 (CA) which provides that s. 13(4)-(7) apply to assignments or licences of communications signals.

[62]   See s. 24(*b*) (CA).

[63]   See s. 25 (CA) which provides that s. 13(4)-(7) apply to assignments or licences of sound recordings.

[64]   See s. 3(1)(*d*) (CA).

[65]   See s. 5(3), (4) (CA).

or musical work. This right may have been assigned to the Canadian Mechanical Reproduction Rights Association ("CMRRA").[66]

If a musical performance is to be communicated in public, the user must also consider applicability of the copyright holder's public performance right.[67] This right may have been assigned to the Society of Composers, Authors and Music Publishers of Canada ("SOCAN").[68] In addition, the copyright holder in a mechanical contrivance also has a rental right in respect of the contrivance (fixation as referred to in this chapter) or any substantial part thereof.[69] Other parties who may have rights to be considered include the holder of the rights in the sound recording and owner of the rights in the communications signal.

All these rights may need to be addressed to properly use the performance in public.

---

[66]   The CMRRA is a collective which administers mechanical reproduction rights on behalf of those rights holders in its repertoire. The CMRRA grants licences for use of these rights. More information on the CMRRA and its licences may be found in *Protection of Copyright and Industrial Design*, Practice Guide (Toronto: Carswell, 1995).

[67]   See s. 3(1) (CA).

[68]   SOCAN is a collective which administers public performance rights on behalf of those rights holders in its repertoire. SOCAN grants licences for use of these rights. More information on SOCAN and its licences may be found in *Protection of Copyright and Industrial Design*, *supra*, footnote 66.

[69]   See s. 5(4)(*c*) (CA).

5

Integrated Circuit Topographies

1. Introduction

Computer technology has had and will continue to have a significant impact on our society and the way in which we interact. At the heart of a computer are one or more semi-conductor chips containing an elaborate and complex three dimensional set of electronic connections. These connections provide the logic, performance, functions and capability of the computer. Considerable investment is made in the design of faster and more efficient semi-conductor chips to drive the demand for greater performance of computer systems.

In the early days of semi-conductor chip design, concern was expressed about how this design effort should be protected. Rather than rely on traditional forms of intellectual property protection, such as copyright law,[1] the United States found it necessary to create a new form of intellectual property to provide framework for the protection of novel mask works used to make integrated circuit designs and the designs themselves.[2]

Canada and other major trading partners of the United States ultimately responded by creating generally similar systems for the protection of this

---

[1] The copyrights which would normally exist in a topography and the mask works used to make the topography were extinguished by s. 64.2(1) (CA).

[2] See *Semi-Conductor Chip Protection Act of 1984*, 17 U.S.C., c. 9. For an electronic version of the Act, see <http://xinfo.ic.gc.ca/>. Note that the United States imposed a requirement on other countries who had sought protection there to implement a similar law. See 17 U.S.C., s. 914 for the provisions providing interim protection while a country implemented the new law. This unilateral approach is inconsistent with a multilateral approach to intellectual property protection and was the subject of criticism.

technology.[3] In Canada, the *Integrated Circuit Topography Act*, S.C. 1990, c. 37, ss. 1-28,[4] addresses the protection of new integrated circuit designs (called a "topography") and integrated circuit products incorporating those designs.

Protection is only available by registering the topography. Failure to file an application within two years of any commercial sale of a product using the topography may result in loss of rights. The rights in a registered topography give the owner a degree of control over subsequent use or dealings with a topography or integrated circuit products incorporating that topography.

2. Scope of Rights

A topography is the design of the interconnections for making an integrated circuit product or the elements, if any, and the interconnections for the making of a customization layer[5] or "layers to be added to an integrated circuit product in an intermediate form".[6] How the design is expressed is irrelevant (*e.g.*, it is not limited to protection of the masks designs in a photo-optical manufacturing process).

The rights in a registered topography may be described as

(a) a reproduction right;

(b) a manufacturing right; and

(c) an exploitation right.

The owner of rights in a registered topography has these rights.

(a) Reproduction Right

The owner of the registered topography has the sole right to reproduce the topography or any substantial part thereof.[7] This gives the owner control over the reproduction of the novel features of the topography.

---

[3] For further background see: "Semi-Conductor Chip Protection in Canada: Proposals for Legislation" prepared by Consumer and Corporate Affairs Canada, April, 1987.

[4] Referred to as "ICTA" throughout the footnotes in this text.

[5] A customization layer is a layer of custom designed electrical connections on a semiconductor chip that permits the designer to customize the functions on the chip for a particular purpose. The customization layer permits the designer to use "standard" functions or routines, designed onto other layers of the chip, with the unique electrical connection on the customization layer, to create the custom chip functions.

[6] See s. 2 (ICTA). An intermediate layer is one or more layers within a semi-conductor chip which have specific functions. The Act permits protection of such parts of a semiconductor chip design.

[7] See s. 3(2)(*a*) (ICTA).

(b) Manufacturing Right

The owner of the registered topography has the sole right to manufacture an integrated circuit product incorporating the topography or any substantial part thereof.[8]

An integrated circuit product is a product that is intended to perform an electronic function and in which the elements, at least one of which is an active element, and some of or all of the interconnections are integrally formed in, on or both in or on a piece of material.[9] The integrated circuit product may be either in a final form or an intermediate form.

(c) Exploitation Right

The owner of the registered topography has the sole right to "import or commercially exploit the topography or any substantial part thereof or an integrated circuit product that incorporates the topography or any substantial part thereof".[10]

The exploitation right permits the owner of the registered topography to seek to control the market for integrated circuit products using the protected topography. This right is subject to exhaustion for a particular integrated circuit product once that product has lawfully been placed into the market.[11]

The full range of remedies is available for an infringement of rights in a registered topography.[12]

The registration of a topography does not give any rights to any "idea, concept, process, system, technique or information that may be embodied in a topography or an integrated circuit product".[13] Many integrated circuit topographies are designed by the creation of multiple optical masks which are, basically, circuit diagrams reflecting the circuit interconnections at each layer of the three dimensional circuit matrix which makes up the integrated circuit topography. Those masks and layouts may be artistic works and might have been protected under copyright law as a result of the labour, skill and judgment incorporated in their design but such protection has been specifically excluded.[14]

---

[8]   See s. 3(2)(*b*) (ICTA).

[9]   See s. 2 (ICTA).

[10]   See s. 3(2)(*c*) (ICTA).

[11]   See s. 6(2)(*c*) (ICTA).

[12]   See s. 9 (ICTA), which provides remedies by way of injunction, payment of royalties, damages, accounts or disposal of any infringing integrated circuit product or any article of which an infringing integrated circuit product forms a part and otherwise is available to the owner of a registered topography.

[13]   See s. 3(3) (ICTA).

[14]   See s. 64.2 (CA).

Computer programs which may be stored on a semi-conductor chip are protected by copyright as literary works.

An inventive algorithm, method or process may be practised by the specific layout of a semi-conductor chip topography. That invention may be separately protected under patent law.

3. Limits on Rights in a Registered Topography

Some limits on the exclusive rights of the owner of a registered topography include:

(a) One may reproduce the topography and/or manufacture an integrated circuit product incorporating the topography for the sole purpose of analysis or evaluation or for teaching or research in respect of topographies.[15]

(b) One may manufacture an integrated circuit product incorporating the topography which was created by means of the analysis or evaluation or research permitted under the Act so long as that topography is original in the sense provided by the Act.[16]

(c) One may import or commercially exploit the topography or an integrated circuit product incorporating the topography but only after that particular integrated circuit topography was sold anywhere by or under the authority of the owner of that right.[17]

(d) One may carry out any of the sole rights of the owner but only if for private and non-commercial purposes.[18]

(e) One may temporarily bring an integrated circuit product incorporating the topography into Canada as part of a vessel, vehicle, aircraft or spacecraft registered in another country if that vehicle enters Canada accidentally, temporarily or for a purpose ancillary to that vehicle.[19]

---

[15] See s. 6(2)(*a*) (ICTA).

[16] See s. 6(2)(*b*) (ICTA). The test of originality is set out in s. 4(2) and (3) (ICTA). This test is discussed below.

[17] See s. 6(2)(*c*) (ICTA). This provides for an exhaustion of the exploitation right once the integrated circuit product incorporating the topography is lawfully placed in the market.

[18] See s. 6(2)(*d*) (ICTA).

[19] See s. 6(2)(*e*) (ICTA). This is a defence similar to that also provided for other forms of intellectual property rights.

(f) One may carry out any of the sole rights of the owner with a topography that is independently created.[20] The defence requires extensive proof of appropriate due diligence in the creation of the independent topography.[21]

(g) No claim for royalties, damages or profits may be commenced more than three years after the infringement occurred.[22] This limitation is qualified by a discovery rule so that the time begins to run from when the plaintiff came to or should have come to have knowledge of the infringement.

4. Types of Things Protected

An integrated circuit product is a product that is intended to perform an electronic function and in which the elements, at least one of which is an active element, and some of or all of the interconnections are integrally formed in, on or both in or on a piece of material.[23] The product may be either in a final form or an intermediate form.

Since use of integrated circuit products is so pervasive and since copyright is likely to apply to the computer programs or data so often stored in such integrated circuit products, one should always address the various rights, if any, in a registered topography and the computer programs or data stored therein.[24]

5. Formal Requirements for Protection

To register a topography one must have:

(a) a registrable topography;

(b) an eligible applicant; and

(c) a complete and proper application form.

A topography must be original to be registrable.[25] For the purposes of the Act a topography is original if:

---

[20] See s. 6(3) (ICTA).

[21] In an American case, *Browntree Corporation v. Advanced Micro Devices Inc.* (1988), 88-1750-E (CM) December 13, 1988 (Calif. D.C.), extensive independent design effort was needed to show independent creation. It is assumed a similar result might operate in Canada.

[22] See s. 12(1) (ICTA).

[23] See s. 2 (ICTA).

[24] See *Apple Computer Inc. v. Mackintosh Computers Ltd.* (1986), 28 D.L.R. (4th) 178 (Fed. T.D.), vard (1987), 16 C.I.P.R. 15 (Fed. C.A.), affd (1990), 71 D.L.R. (4th) 95 (S.C.C.), for a case recognizing the copyright protection of computer programs stored on read only memory (ROM) semi-conductor chips. See also s. 33 (ICTA) and s. 64.2(2) (CA), preserving such rights.

[25] See s. 4(1)(*a*) (ICTA).

(a) it has not been created by "mere reproduction of another topography",[26] and

(b) it is the result of intellectual effort.[27]

The topography cannot be commonplace at the time created.[28] A combination of commonplace elements can be original if the combination satisfies the above tests.[29]

In order for the topography to be registrable, the creator of it must have been an individual or business with a real and effective establishment for creation of topographies in Canada or be a national of another country and make a claim under an applicable international treaty between that country and Canada.[30]

In order to be registrable, the application for registration of the topography must have been filed in Canada before the topography is commercially exploited anywhere or within two years thereafter.[31]

6. Term of Protection

The rights in a registered topography last for ten years after the earlier of the calender year of the filing date of the application or the calender year of the first commercial exploitation of the topography.[32]

7. Ownership of the Rights

The creator owns the rights to a topography. Where the creator made the topography in the course of employment or pursuant to a contract, the employer or party to the agreement is deemed to be the creator unless there is an agreement to the contrary.[33] The right of the creator may be assigned to another.

---

[26]   See s. 4(2)(*a*) (ICTA).

[27]   See s. 4(2)(*b*) (ICTA).

[28]   See s. 4(2)(*b*) (ICTA).

[29]   See s. 4(3) (ICTA).

[30]   See s. 4(1)(*c*) (ICTA).

[31]   See s. 4(1)(*b*) (ICTA). This limitation may be waived if the first commercial exploitation occurred in Canada. See s. 4(4) (ICTA).

[32]   See s. 5 (ICTA).

[33]   See ss. 2(4) and 3(1) (ICTA).

The owner of rights in a topography may grant or transfer any rights in the topography or a portion thereof.[34] Assignments or licences may be registered.[35]

8. Special Rules

Failure to file an application within two years of any commercial sale of a product using the topography may result in loss of rights.

There is a special defence of innocent infringement available.[36] This defence is not available if the containers housing the integrated circuit products, which contain the topography, are marked with a title substantially the same as that which appears on the register.[37]

Protection of a topography requires registration in each country in which protection is sought. An international treaty provides a basis for mutual recognition of such rights.[38]

---

[34]   See s. 7(1) and (2) (ICTA).

[35]   See s. 21(1) (ICTA).

[36]   See ss. 10 and 11(1) (ICTA).

[37]   See s. 11(2) (ICTA).

[38]   See *Treaty on the Protection of Intellectual Property in respect of Integrated Circuits*, W.I.P.O., Geneva, IPIC/CE/II/2, March 17, 1986. See also 17 U.S.C., ss. 902 and 914 for provisions providing a basis for protection of rights of foreigners (*i.e.*, including Canadians) in the United States.

6

Industrial Design

1. Introduction

Industrial design law relates to the protection of the appearance of objects or articles made in quantities of more than fifty and which are based on designs which are addressed to the shape, pattern or ornamentation of the objects or articles. Certain designs of two or three dimensional shapes, patterns or ornamentation are not protectable under copyright law if more than fifty copies of an article bearing such design are made.[1] Some, but not all, of those designs may be protectable under industrial design law.[2] The relationship between copyright and industrial design law is quite complex.[3]

The term "industrial design" itself is not defined in either the *Copyright Act* or *Industrial Design Act*, R.S.C. 1985, c. I-9.[4] The meaning applied by the courts has been that industrial designs are original configurations, shapes, patterns or ornamentation which are applied to a useful article of manufacture and which appeal to the eye.

---

[1] See s. 64.2 (CA).

[2] There appears to have been a public policy behind the separate protection of such designs at a time when England had a cumbersome registry system of copyright which applied to only certain limited works. When the copyright system was reformed, the industrial design system remained in its more ancient form. As a result, designers of certain works get automatic copyright protection and designers of other works get no protection or only the limited ability to seek protection under the industrial design system. Given the present automatic and inclusive copyright system it is difficult to see what broad public policy goals are served by discriminating against designers in certain industries or sectors.

[3] The copyright – industrial design interface is discussed in Section 8, "Special Rules", *infra*.

[4] Note that all future footnote references to the *Industrial Design Act* will be indicated by "IDA" following the section number. For an electronic version of the Act, see <http://xinfo.ic.gc.ca/>.

Unlike copyright, but similar to patents and integrated circuit topographies, the industrial design system requires registration in each country in order to create enforceable rights. Industrial design registration is available to protect aesthetic features of an article or product. Industrial design law is intended to provide protection for features of shape, configuration and ornament applied to an article or product.

The rights in a registered design give the owner a degree of control over subsequent use or dealings with a design or articles embodying that design. Failure to file an application within one year of any public use, disclosure or sale of the design or a product or process bearing the design may result in loss of rights.

2. Scope of Rights

A design means those features of shape, configuration, pattern or ornament and any combination of those features which may be applied to an article. In a finished article those features must appeal to the eye.[5]

(a) Manufacturing Right

The owner of the registered design has the sole right to manufacture an article incorporating the design or any substantial part thereof.[6]

(b) Exploitation Right

The owner of the registered design has the sole right to import for the purpose of trade or business, sell or rent an article incorporating the design or any substantial part thereof.[7] These rights include the exclusive right to offer or expose for sale the article to which the design has been applied. Further, the owner of the rights in a registered design can also exercise those rights in relation to a kit which one can use to assemble the article.[8]

The full range of remedies are available for an infringement of rights in a registered design.[9]

The registration of a design does not extend to any method or principle of construction that may be embodied in a design or an article.[10] Similarly, a

---

[5]   See s. 2 (IDA).

[6]   See s. 11(1)(*a*) (IDA).

[7]   See s. 11(1)(*a*) (IDA).

[8]   See s. 11(1)(*b*) (IDA).

[9]   See s. 15.1 (IDA), which provides remedies by way of injunction, damages, accounts or disposal of any infringing article or kit.

[10]   See s. 5.1(*b*) (IDA). See also *Angelstone Ltd. v. Artistic Stone Ltd.*, [1960] Ex. C.R. 286 (Ex. Ct.), which found the registration of the design of a construction block invalid as an effort to obtain a monopoly on an article of manufacture itself and not the ornamentation

registered design does not extend to any useful features embodied in a design or an article.[11]

The rights in a registered industrial design are separate and apart from the rights in the article to which the design is applied.

3. Limits on Rights in a Registered Design

Some limits on the exclusive rights of the owner of a registered design include:

(a) Unless a proper notice is used on the article or its container,[12] innocent infringement is a defence and does not permit the owner of the registered design to obtain any relief other than injunctive relief.[13]

(b) The Act only protects the design or a substantially similar design applied to an article.[14] In applying this test the court may consider the degree of similarity of the registered design to other previously published designs.

(c) One may use useful features embodied in a design or an article.[15]

(d) One may use any method or principle of construction that may be embodied in a design or an article.[16]

An action in respect of infringement of rights in a registered design must be commenced within three years of the infringing act in order to obtain a remedy at law.[17]

4. Types of Things Protected

An article is defined to mean a product that is intended to perform a useful function.[18] A useful function is one which serves a function other than merely serving as the substrate or carrier for artistic or literary matter.[19] Industrial designs are original configurations, shapes, patterns or ornamentation which are applied to a useful article of manufacture and which appeal to the eye.

---

of such an article. Note, however, that a design can relate to the external shape of an article: See *Cimon Ltd. v. Bench Made Furniture Corp.* (1964), 30 Fox Pat. C. 77 (Ex. Ct.).

[11]   See s. 5.1(*a*) (IDA).

[12]   See Section 8, *infra*, for details of notices.

[13]   See s. 17(1) (IDA).

[14]   See s. 11(2) (IDA).

[15]   See s. 5.1(*a*) (IDA).

[16]   See s. 5.1(*b*) (IDA).

[17]   See s. 18 (IDA).

[18]   See s. 2 (IDA).

[19]   See s. 2 (IDA).

Examples of industrial designs might include the shape of a coffee cup, chair, the shape or appearance of a fender of an automobile, the shape of a type of nut cracker,[20] the shape of a boat hull,[21] the appearance of a telephone desk set or soap container. Other examples might include decorations or patterns applied to an object, such as an item of furniture[22] or cutlery. A purely useful article or method of manufacture may not be subject to industrial design protection.[23]

Note that the design itself may be a work normally subject to copyright protection. In certain circumstances copyright protection is excluded for certain works.[24] In most such cases the only protection available to the designer, if at all, may be industrial design registration. The relationship between copyright and industrial design is discussed in Section 8, "Special Rules", *infra*.

5. Formal Requirements for Protection

Industrial design protection is only available under a registry system.[25] Rights only arise on registration of the design. To register a design one must have:

(a) a registrable design;

(b) an eligible applicant; and

(c) a complete and proper application form.

(a) Registrable Designs

To be registrable, certain formal conditions must be satisfied in order to come within the protection of the *Industrial Design Act*. These conditions are:

---

[20]   See, for example, *Re Industrial Design Registration No. 43,273* (1977), 45 C.P.R. (2d) 238 (Pat. App. Bd. & Pat. Commr.).

[21]   See the controversial decision in *Bayliner Marine Corp. v. Doral Boats Ltd.* (1985), 5 C.I.P.R. 268 (Fed. T.D.), revd (1986), 10 C.P.R. (3d) 289 (Fed. C.A.) which, in an effort to exclude copyright protection for a boat hull design copied by the defendant, the court amended regulations under the Act resulting in a substantially reduced scope of protection available under industrial design law to all designers.

[22]   See, for example, *Cimon Ltd. v. Bench Made Furniture Corp.* (1964), 30 Fox Pat. C. 77 (Ex. Ct.).

[23]   See *Angelstone Ltd. v. Artistic Stone Ltd.*, [1960] Ex. C.R. 286 (Ex. Ct.), regarding an effort to protect a form of building block.

[24]   See Section 8(b), "Relationship between Copyright and Industrial Design", *infra*, for more detail on the interface between copyright and industrial design. See also s. 64(2) (CA).

[25]   For more details on the registration process including a step-by-step guide to registration of an industrial design see *Protection of Copyright and Industrial Design*, Practice Guide (Toronto: Carswell, 1995).

(a) the design must have aesthetic appeal;

(b) the work must be original;

(c) the design must satisfy requirements of novelty; and

(d) the design must not be contrary to public morality or order.[26]

(b) Novelty and Originality

A design must be original and novel to be registrable.[27] For the purposes of the Act, a design is original if:

(a) it is not identical with any design already registered,[28] and

(b) it does not so closely resemble any other design already registered as to be confusing therewith.[29]

"Original" for industrial designs means that the design must be the exercise of intellectual activity so as to suggest for the first time the application of a particular pattern, shape or ornament to some subject-matter where it has not been applied before.[30] The degree of originality is greater than that required for copyright.[31]

To be original, the design must emanate from the designer. It must be the product of the designer's intellectual activity. Industrial design is only concerned with the aesthetic appeal and so it is the eye-appealing features which must be new. The ideas or article underlying the design need not be original.

The test used in comparing a design with a prior design involves the following steps:

1. Examine each of the articles (to which the design is applied) separately.

2. Look at the design as a whole.

3. Determine whether the need is for a substantial, not trivial or infinitesimal change.[32]

---

[26] See s. 6(2) (IDA).

[27] See ss. 4(1)(*b*) and 6(1) (IDA).

[28] See s. 6(1) (IDA).

[29] See s. 6(1) (IDA).

[30] *Clatworthy & Son Ltd. v. Dale Display Fixtures Ltd.*, [1929] S.C.R. 429.

[31] See *Bata Industries Ltd. v. Warrington Inc.* (1985), 5 C.P.R. (3d) 339 (Fed. T.D.).

[32] See *Re Application for Plastic Bottle for Liquid Soaps* (1977), 46 C.P.R. (2d) 208 (Pat. App. Bd. & Pat. Commr.).

In addition, to be registrable, an application for registration of an industrial design must have been filed no less than one year after the design has been published:

(a) in Canada for applications filed before January 1, 1994, and

(b) in Canada or elsewhere for applications filed on or after January 1, 1994.[33]

The industrial design application must be forwarded to the Industrial Design Office within one year of the design being made public in Canada. Failure to make application for the industrial design within one year of any publication may result in loss of rights.[34] Foreign rights may be lost by any public exposure to the design before the application is filed.

(c) Aesthetic Appeal

Industrial design law is only intended to protect design features which appeal to the eye. Ornamentation is not the same as beauty. It is sufficient that ornamentation serves to distinguish an article's appearance.[35] There is no requirement for aesthetic appeal of the design or the article bearing the design.

The features of the design must be visible to the user when used or perceived.

(d) Eligible Applicant

The author of the design may be a national or resident of Canada or of another country. The owner of the rights in the design, including a successor in title to the original designer, may make application for registration of the design. Nationals of Paris Convention countries can make a claim under that treaty.[36]

6. Term of Protection

An industrial design is registered for ten years.[37] This period runs from registration of the design. Prior to January 1, 1994, the term of registration was five years and that registration was capable of being renewed for a further five-year term.[38]

---

[33]   See s. 6(3) (IDA).

[34]   See s. 6(3) (IDA).

[35]   See *DRG Inc. v. Datafile Ltd.* (1991), 35 C.P.R. (3d) 243 (Fed. C.A.).

[36]   See s. 29 (IDA). See also Chapter 14, "International Treaties", for a discussion of these and other treaty provisions.

[37]   See s. 10 (IDA).

[38]   See s. 29.1(1) (IDA).

Similar to the patent system, maintenance fees are payable by the owner of a registered design. Failure to pay these fees can result in a premature end of the registration term.[39]

7. Ownership of the Rights

The basic principle is that the designer (author) is the owner (proprietor) of the design. Only the owner may apply for and obtain registration of the industrial design.[40]

If a design is made for both good and valuable consideration, the person ordering the design will be the owner of the design rights.[41] If the parties enter into a written agreement specifically addressing the ownership of the rights in the industrial design, the courts will give force to that agreement.[42] The right of the designer may be assigned to another but the assignment must be registered in the Industrial Design Office.[43]

The owner of rights in a design may grant any rights in the design or a portion thereof by licence.[44] A licence must also be registered in the Industrial Design Office.

8. Special Rules

(a) Marking

The rights of an owner of an industrial design registration may be substantially enhanced by proper use and placement of an appropriate notice on each article to which the design is applied.

There is a special defence of innocent infringement available.[45] This defence is not available if the containers housing the articles which contain the design are marked with a title substantially the same as that which appears on the register.[46] Unless a proper notice is used on the article or its container, the innocent infringement defence does not permit the owner of the registered design to obtain any relief other than injunctive relief.[47]

---

[39] See s. 10(2) (IDA).

[40] See *Uniformes Town & Country Inc. v. Labrie* (1989), 24 C.P.R. (3d) 162 (Fed. T.D.); *Comstock Canada v. Electec Ltd.* (1991), 38 C.P.R. (3d) 29 (Fed. T.D.).

[41] See s. 12 (IDA).

[42] See s. 4(1) (IDA).

[43] See s. 13(1) (IDA).

[44] See s. 13(2) (IDA).

[45] See ss. 10 and 11(1) (IDA).

[46] See s. 11(2) (IDA).

[47] See s. 17(1) (IDA).

The innocent infringement defence is not available if at the time of the alleged infringing act the owner of the registered design can show that a proper mark or notice was placed on or in association with the articles incorporating the design.[48] Proper notice would include one of the following:

(a) the capital letter D in a circle together with the name or usual abbreviation of the name of the owner of the registered design; or

(b) if the design was registered before June 9, 1993[49] and was a woven fabric, the letters "Rd." or "Enr." or both "Rd." and "Enr." together with the name of the owner of the registered design[50] at one end of the article; or

(c) if the design was registered before June 9, 1993 and was manufactured with a substance other than a woven fabric, the letters "Rd." or "Enr." or both "Rd." and "Enr." together with the name of the owner of the registered design[51] and the year of registration on the edge or other convenient part of the article. In the cases of article not of woven fabric, the notice or mark may be applied to the material itself or to a label attached to the article.[52]

This notice should be marked on all or substantially all of the articles to which the registration pertains that are or were distributed in Canada.[53] The notice may also be applied to a label or packaging attached to or associated with such articles.

(b) Relationship between Copyright and Industrial Design

Works which may be considered for an industrial design application may also be artistic works normally protected by copyright. There is a complex relationship between the *Copyright Act* and the *Industrial Design Act* and their respective regulations. Copyright and industrial design protection each have advantages and disadvantages. Because of the way in which the courts have, on occasion, interpreted this area of law and due to the lack of substantial case law on the subject since the 1993 reforms, it is often difficult to confirm whether or not either or both systems are applicable. Many prudent applicants seek to assert a claim for *both* forms of protection.

---

[48] See s. 17(2) (IDA).

[49] Prior to enactment of the *Intellectual Property Improvement Act*, S.C. 1993, c. 15, on June 9, 1993, it was mandatory to mark an article bearing a registered industrial design in order to enforce that registration against a third party. The reform now makes the placement of a notice optional but provides presumptions which facilitate the owner's ability to bring enforcement action by placing the notice on the articles.

[50] See ss. 29.1(2) and 30(5) (IDA).

[51] See ss. 29.1(2) and 30(5) (IDA).

[52] See ss. 29.1(3) and 30(6) (IDA).

[53] See s. 17(2)(*a*) and (*b*) (IDA).

The following comments seek to introduce some of the more significant features of the interrelationship between industrial design law and copyright law in Canada.

Canada's first legislation in respect of industrial designs was *An Act to Amend the Act Respecting Trade Marks, and to Provide for the Registration of Designs.*[54] This Act was based on an even earlier English statute dealing with registered designs. In those early days, copyright protection was generally assumed to be available only for artistic and literary works. There was some concern that copyright protection should not be available for artistic works (designs) which could be mass produced. As a result, a separate system was set up for certain designs which were intended to be mass produced. This system finds its culmination in our present *Industrial Design Act.*

In an age where useful works, such as computer programs, or highly commercial works, such as musical works are protected with all the advantages of copyright, one might question whether this discrimination is still justified.

Some important revisions were made to the *Industrial Design Act* in the 1988 reforms.[55] Specifically, s. 46 of the *Copyright Act* was repealed and replaced with the following section.

64. (1) In this section and section 64.1,

"article" means any thing that is made by hand, tool or machine;

"design" means features of shape, configuration, pattern or ornament and any combination of those features that, in a finished article, appeal to and are judged solely by the eye;

"useful article" means an article that has a utilitarian function and includes a model of any such article;

"utilitarian function", in respect of an article, means a function other than merely serving as a substrate or carrier for artistic or literary matter.

(2) Where copyright subsists in a design applied to a useful article or in an artistic work from which the design is derived and, by or under the authority of any person who owns the copyright in Canada or who owns the copyright elsewhere,

(*a*)   the article is reproduced in a quantity of more than fifty, or

(*b*)   where the article is a plate, engraving or cast, the article is used for producing more than fifty useful articles,

---

[54]   S.C. 1861, c. 21.

[55]   See *An Act to Amend the Copyright Act and other Acts in Consequence Thereof*, S.C. 1988, c. 65 on June 7, 1988. In certain cases it may be necessary to review the relationship of copyright and industrial design law prior to June, 1988. For more details on the law prior to these reforms see *Protection of Copyright and Industrial Design*, *supra*, footnote 25.

it shall not thereafter be an infringement of the copyright or the moral rights for anyone

> (*c*) to reproduce the design of the article or a design not differing substantially from the design of the article by
>
> > (i) making the article, or
> >
> > (ii) making a drawing or other reproduction in any material form of the article, or
>
> (*d*) to do with an article, drawing or reproduction that is made as described in paragraph (*c*) anything that the owner of the copyright has the sole right to do with the design or artistic work in which the copyright subsists.

(3) Subsection (2) does not apply in respect of the copyright or the moral rights in an artistic work in so far as the work is used as or for

> (*a*) a graphic or photographic representation that is applied to the face of an article;
>
> (*b*) a trade-mark or a representation thereof or a label;
>
> (*c*) material that has a woven or knitted pattern or that is suitable for piece goods or surface coverings or for making wearing apparel;
>
> (*d*) an architectural work that is a building or a model of a building;
>
> (*e*) a representation of a real or fictitious being, event or place that is applied to an article as a feature of shape, configuration, pattern or ornament;
>
> (*f*) articles that are sold as a set, unless more than fifty sets are made; or
>
> (*g*) such other work or article as may be prescribed by regulation.

(4) Subsections (2) and (3) apply only in respect of designs created after the coming into force of this subsection, and section 64 of this Act and the *Industrial Design Act*, as they read immediately before the coming into force of this subsection, as well as the rules made under them, continue to apply in respect of designs created before that coming into force.

The 1988 amendment had a significant impact on the relationship between the *Industrial Design Act* and the *Copyright Act*.

Note that s. 64(2) is only relevant where - with the authority of the copyright holder - the article is reproduced in a quantity of more than fifty or where the article is a plate, engraving or cast used for producing more than fifty useful articles.

The exclusion from copyright is not absolute. It applies only if the mass production occurred with the owner's consent or authority. The design may continue to be protected by copyright except that the copyright holder may not be able to bring a copyright infringement action to prevent the reproduction of a particular article which has been reproduced in a quantity of more than fifty. This means, for example, where a particular design may have a number of applications, copyright may continue to exist in that design. Industrial design protection would be available for the application of that design in a particular article which satisfies the requirements of s. 64(2).

The exclusion in s. 64(2) is subject to the further exemptions in s. 64(3). That subsection specifically exempts from the operation of that section (and hence returns to the field of copyright protection) a list of subject-matter which would otherwise be captured under s. 64(2). Note s. 64(3)(g) indicates that the list can be extended by regulation. A useful strategy for an industry that would prefer copyright protection instead of industrial design protection may be to lobby the federal government to exclude that industry's works or designs from the operation of the *Industrial Design Act* by having them included in a regulation under s. 64(3)(g).[56]

(c) International Priority

By virtue of the Convention for the Protection of Industrial Property made in Paris (Paris Convention)[57] an applicant for industrial design protection may file a corresponding application in the appropriate government office of other member countries and claim the priority of the first filing date but only if such subsequent filings are made within six months of the first filing date. Canadian applicants making their first filing for a design must therefore be aware that foreign applications filed up to six months before the Canadian application is filed may have priority to obtain the registration for the design.[58] Entitlement under the Paris Convention or otherwise to file industrial design applications in foreign countries are or may be prejudiced by any public exposure to the design before the first filing was made.

---

[56]   It is important to note the consequences of s. 64(3) and the reforms introduced by it. In a number of cases, for certain types of articles, the protection available has been switched from industrial design to copyright or vice versa. As a result, there are a number of strategies which are available to designers depending on whether they wish to seek protection under copyright or under industrial design law. These strategies might include:

> (1) Where the work was protected by copyright before the 1988 reform but would be protected by industrial design registration after the reform, and copyright was preferred as the form of protection, the product or works protected by copyright should not be modified;

> (2) Where a design was protected by industrial design before reform and would now be protected by copyright, and copyright was preferred as the form of protection, then a design should be substantially redesigned or modified; or

> (3) Where possible and if copyright protection was preferred, an applicant might seek to apply political pressure to have their goods or class of goods excluded by the regulations.

[57]   Some more details on the Paris Convention and use of convention priority may be found in Chapter 14, "International Treaties".

[58]   See s. 29 (IDA).

7

Trade-marks

1. Introduction

A trade-mark is a way of distinguishing one trader's product or service from that of another trader. Trade-marks can be in various forms (see Section 4, "Types of Things Protected", *infra*). Canada's law is based on the premise that the function of a trade-mark is to indicate the source or origin of a trader's products or services. Primarily a trade-mark distinguishes the products or services of one trader from those of another.[1] The role of trade-marks is increasingly evolving to keep pace with the growth of licensing and franchise operations.

Trade-marks protect the goodwill and reputation associated with a product[2] or service. Trade-mark law provides essentially no protection for the ideas or concept underlying the technology, product or service associated with the trade-mark except that certain well-known shapes may be protected as distinguishing guises, a form of trade-mark.

Unlike other forms of intellectual property, no trademark rights arise on creation of the trade-mark. Rather it is the *use* of the trade-mark which gives rise to enforceable rights. Since the right does not arise from intellectual activity, some commentators do not categorize trade-marks as intellectual property. On the other hand, trade-mark rights are closely allied with several forms of intellectual property (such as copyrights, moral and plant breeders' rights); are intangible (like other forms of intellectual property); and are

---

[1] This broader view is the basis of modern U.S. trade-mark law. See, for example, the Federal Trademark Dilution Act, 15 U.S.C. 1125, which provides a dilution remedy to owners of famous marks, and Schecter, *The Rational Basis of Trademark Protection* (1927), 40 Harv. L. Rev. 813 for the basis of such a remedy.

[2] The *Trade-marks Act*, R.S.C. 1985, c. T-13, refers to wares. The terms products or wares are used interchangeably in this text. Note that all future footnote references to the *Trade-marks Act* will be indicated by "T-MA" following the section number. For an electronic version of the Act, see <http://xinfo.ic.gc.ca/>.

enforced using similar remedies (and often in the same forum) as other forms of intellectual property.

There are three broad areas or systems of law providing some degree of protection of trade-marks and reputation. These areas of law deal with the protection of registered trade-marks (discussed in this chapter), the protection of unregistered trade-marks,[3] and the protection of rights in personality.[4]

Registered trade-marks are protected under the *Trade-marks Act*. Trade-marks, including unregistered trade-marks, may also receive a level of protection under the common law passing off action, the provisions of s. 7 of the Act, or under certain specialized torts such as appropriation of personality. Other remedies may be available depending on the circumstances.

2. Scope of Rights

Trade-marks may be registered under the provisions of the *Trade-marks Act*.[5] A registered trade-mark provides the owner with an exclusive national right to use the trade-mark in association with the products or services for which it was registered as well as special remedies under the Act.[6]

The registration of the trade-mark provides the following rights:

(a) an exclusive right to use the trade-mark;

(b) a right to be free of use of a confusingly similar trade-mark by another; and

(c) a right to be free of use of the registered trade-mark by another in a manner which may depreciate the goodwill attached thereto.

---

[3] Unregistered trade-marks may obtain a degree of protection under the common law passing off action and s. 7 (T-MA). See Chapter 8, "Protection of Unregistered Trade-marks", for more details of this form of protection.

[4] Rights in a person's likeness, voice, appearance, shape or other attributes of personality may obtain a degree of protection under the common law and certain provisions of privacy legislation in some provinces. See Chapter 9, "Personality Rights", for more details of this form of protection. In some cases copyright law (Chapter 2), moral rights (Chapter 3) and/or neighbouring rights (Chapter 4) may also play a role in protecting rights in a person's likeness, voice or other attributes of the person's personality.

[5] Details on making a trade-mark application may be found in White, *Selection and Protecting Trade-marks*, Canada Practice Guide (Toronto: Carswell, 1994).

[6] For internet issues including domain name problems, see Gahtan, Kratz, Mann, *Internet Law*, (Carswell, 1998).

(a) Exclusive Use

The owner of the registered trade-mark has the sole right throughout Canada to use the trade-mark in association with the products and/or services for which it was registered.[7]

"Use" for trade-marks purposes means in relation to products, the placement of the trade-mark on the product or on packaging for the product at the point of sale or when possession is passed to the customer of the product,[8] or in relation to services, the use of the trade-mark incidental to the provision of the services or use in advertising the ability to provide the services.[9]

(b) Confusion

The owner of the registered trade-mark has the right to be free of any use of a confusingly similar trade-mark or trade-name.[10]

The test for confusion is whether the ordinary customer or unwary purchaser would believe the product or service of one trader is likely to be related to the product or service of another trader.[11] One considers the overall impression of the trade-marks and any words associated with the trade-marks.

Section 6 of the *Trade-marks Act*[12] sets out a number of factors which may be considered in determining whether the trade-marks are confusing. Those factors are:

(a) the inherent distinctiveness of the trade-marks or trade-names and the extent to which they have become known;[13]

(b) the length of time the trade-marks or trade-names have been in use;[14]

(c) the nature of the wares, services or business;[15]

---

[7]   Section 19 (T-MA).

[8]   Subsection 4(1) (T-MA).

[9]   Subsection 4(2) (T-MA).

[10]   See s. 20 (T-MA).

[11]   See, for example, *Rowntree Co. v. Paulin Chambers Co.*, [1968] S.C.R. 134, 54 C.P.R. 43.

[12]   See specifically s. 6(5) for factors which may be considered in the determination of confusion.

[13]   See s. 6(5)(*a*) (T-MA). Inherently distinctive trade-marks are generally trade-marks that convey no meaning other than that provided by the trade-mark owner. Examples are made-up words such as XEROX or EXXON which have been adopted as trade-marks. Inherently distinctive trade-marks are entitled to a higher level of protection.

[14]   See s. 6(5)(*b*) (T-MA). The length of time the trade-mark or trade-names have been in use may affect the extent of reputation the trade-mark has obtained. Extensive long-term use of the two marks together where there has been no actual confusion suggests there is no confusion.

[15]   See s. 6(5)(*c*) (T-MA). Confusion is more likely if the wares, services or business with which both trade-marks or trade-names are associated are the same. For example, ESCO

(d) the nature of the trade;[16]

(e) the degree of resemblance between the trade-marks or trade-names in appearance or sound or in the ideas suggested by them.[17]

(c) Depreciation of Goodwill

The owner of the registered trade-mark has the right to be free of use of the trade-mark in a manner which is likely to have the effect of depreciating the value of the goodwill attached thereto.[18]

This provides the possibility of a further remedy in addition to those provided by ss. 19 and 20 when a registered trade-mark is used by another in a manner likely to have the effect of depreciating the value of the goodwill attached to the trade-mark. In order for s. 22 to apply, the defendant must be using the trade-mark as registered. The use must be "use" within the meaning of the Act. "Use" is defined as a mark which is used by a person for the purpose of distinguishing his wares or services from those of others. If the use of a trade-mark is not trade-mark "use" then it may be possible for the defendant to escape statutory liability since the defendant may not be using the trade-mark as a trade-mark within the meaning of the Act.[19]

---

and ESCONE were found to be confusing, both being used for clothing. Consumers tend to pay more attention to costly products than inexpensive items. As a result, smaller changes between two trade-marks or trade-names in respect of expensive products may not result in confusion.

[16]   See s. 6(5)(*d*) (T-MA). If both trade-marks or trade-names are used in the same channels of trade, the likelihood of confusion is high. Other factors in this regard include whether or not wares are both sold at retail, wholesale or other trade level.

[17]   See s. 6(5)(*e*) (T-MA). The degree of resemblance between the trade-marks is a significant factor. The resemblance may be in appearance, *e.g.*, CAVALIER for soft drinks or CAVALIER for fruit juice, in sound, *e.g.*, ESCO or ESCONE for clothing, or in ideas suggested by them, *e.g.*, CLEANX or CLEAREX for cleaners.

[18]   See s. 22 (T-MA). Also relevant is s. 22(2) which provides that in an action respecting use of a trade-mark contrary to s. 22(1), the court may decline to order the recovery of damages or profits and may permit the defendant to continue to sell wares marked with the trade-mark that were in the defendant's possession or control at the time notice was given that the owner of the registered trade-mark had complained of trade-mark use.

[19]   The expression goodwill and depreciating the value of goodwill have been interpreted in *Clairol International Corp. v. Thomas Supply & Equipment Co.*, 55 C.P.R. 176, [1968] 2 Ex. C.R. 552 (Ex. Ct.), as follows:

> . . . to produce and in some way take advantage of the reputation and connection . . . to take away a whole or summation of the custom otherwise to be expected and to make it less extensive and thus less advantageous. . . . goodwill has value only to the extent the advantage of the reputation and connection which its owner enjoys and whatever reduces that advantage reduces the value of it. Depreciation of that value . . . occurs whether it arises through reduction of the esteem of which the mark itself is held or through the direct persuasion or enticing of customers who could otherwise be expected to buy or continue to buy goods bearing the trade-mark.

A side-by-side comparison of the products using trade-marks at the point of sale is likely to result in liability. In *Interlego AG v. Irwin Toy Ltd.,*[20] a proceeding was brought for an interlocutory injunction. It was held that the display by a competitor of a registered trade-mark on packaging and references to such trade-mark in retail catalogues for purposes of carrying the competitor's ware with the wares covered by the registered trade-mark constituted use of the trade-mark as contemplated by the Act. Such use violated the exclusive rights of the registered owner to use the trade-mark as provided for in s. 22.

A disclaimer may aid in avoiding liability where use of a competitor's trade-mark is to inform the customer of the compatibility of the defendant's product. In *Nintendo of America Inc. v. Camerica Corp.,*[21] the defendant advertised and put on the market a device to be used with video games. On the package it was stated that the defendant's device worked with the plaintiff's video games but the packaging had a disclaimer of any association with the plaintiff's device.

In the case of services, a competitor's trade-mark relating to similar services would be used within the meaning of s. 4(2) if displayed in the *performance of the service or in the advertising of that service.* For services, mere advertising for a service in association with a trade-mark is use of that trade-mark. There is no requirement that there is any transfer of property which is fundamental to the nature of wares but not services.[22]

(d) Right to Authorize Others

In addition to the sole rights of the trade-mark owner, the owner of the registered trade-mark also has the right to authorize others to carry out any of the acts contemplated by those sole rights.[23] The 1993 reforms purport to act retrospectively providing that use by a licensee is deemed always to have

---

[20]   (1985), 3 C.P.R. (3d) 476, 4 C.I.P.R. 1 (Fed. T.D.).

[21]   (1991), 42 F.T.R. 12, 34 C.P.R. (3d) 193, affd (1991), 36 C.P.R. (3d) 352 (Fed. C.A.).

[22]   In *Eye Masters Ltd. v. Ross King Holdings Ltd.* (1992), 4 C.P.R. (3d) 214 (Fed. T.D.) (interim injunction); 44 C.P.R. (3d) 459, [1992] 3 F.C. 625 (Fed. T.D.) (interlocutory injunction), the plaintiff sought an interlocutory injunction to restrain the defendant from referring to the plaintiff's trade-mark in comparison advertising. Both the defendant and plaintiff were engaged in the retail sale of eyeglasses. The defendant's view was that the plaintiff charged higher prices for the products being sold and the defendant's advertising focused on this view. While the Court was skeptical regarding the broader protection which appears to be provided by s. 4(2), it granted an interlocutory injunction.

[23]   See s. 50 (T-MA). Note that the ability to license use of a trade-mark to others is, strictly speaking, contrary to the source theory of trade-mark law. Under law in force as recently as June 8, 1993, the owner of a registered trade-mark could only permit others to use the trade-mark if a registered user's appointment was filed at the Trade-marks Office. Failure to take this precaution would result in loss of the registration for the trade-mark. The reforms introduced in 1993 permit licensing of trade-marks.

been use by the trade-mark owner. There is a catch,[24] however, the trade-mark licence need not be recorded in the Trade-marks Office.

The former provisions were considered to indicate that a licence for use of a trade-mark could only be granted directly to a licensee. This inhibited certain types of distribution and marketing activities. The new law softens the previous apparent restrictions on sublicensing of trade-marks. The new provision states that a trade-mark licence may be granted by or *under the authority* of the trade-mark owner. Further, the requirement for control by the owner of the trade-mark can be direct or indirect. It is suggested that appropriate terms in a head licence agreement should give the owner at least indirect control over use of the trade-mark by a sublicensee.

3. Limits on Trade-mark Enforcement

Some substantial defences or limits on the enforceability of a registered trade-mark are:

(a) any defect in registration;[25]

(b) any adverse change in the distinctiveness of the trade-mark;[26]

(c) loss of distinctiveness through unlicensed use of the trade-mark by others;[27]

---

[24]   Under s. 50(1) (T-MA), the trade-mark owner must have an ability to control the character and quality of the wares and/or services provided by the sublicensee in association with the trade-marks. The control may be direct or indirect.

[25]   See Section 5, "Formal Requirements for Registration", *infra*, which describes the requirements for registration of a trade-mark in Canada.

[26]   See, for example, s. 12(1)(*b*) (T-MA), which requires that the trade-mark not be descriptive of the wares or services it is associated with. See, for example, *Canadian Shredded Wheat Co. v. Kellogg Co. of Canada*, [1938] 1 All E.R. 618, [1938] 2 D.L.R. 145 (Ont. P.C.), which found SHREDDED WHEAT to be an apt description of the defendant's product. Over time a trade-mark may become descriptive, not distinctive, of the wares or services with which it is associated. See also *Staffordshire Properties Ltd. v. Canada (Registrar of Trade Marks)* (1976), 26 C.P.R. (2d) 134 (Fed. T.D.) for a case finding KILNCRAFT descriptive of the fact the wares were produced using a kiln; for a case where a challenge is made to an existing trademark registration alleging it has become descriptive and hence unregistrable over time, see *Aladdin Industries Inc. v. Canadian Thermos Products Ltd.* (1969), 57 C.P.R. 230, [1969] 2 Ex. C.R. 80, 41 Fox Pat. C. 26, affd (1972), 6 C.P.R. (2d) 1 (S.C.C.).

[27]   Since a trade-mark must distinguish the wares or services of its owner, use of the same trade-mark by another trader for essentially the same wares or services would result in the trade-mark becoming no longer distinctive of the original owner's wares or services. Exceptions are use licensed under s. 50 (T-MA) or use by infringers where the owner takes reasonably prompt action to restrain such unauthorized use.

(d) failure to use the trade-mark;[28] and

(e) failure to bring action within the applicable limitation period.[29] An action claiming prior use as an attack on the registered trade-mark must be brought within five years of the registration of the trade-mark.[30]

The full range of remedies are available for an infringement of trade-mark.[31] An action for infringement of a registered trade-mark may be brought in either the Federal Court or in a provincial court of superior jurisdiction. An action to expunge or amend a registration of a trade-mark must be brought in the Federal Court.

4. Types of Things Protected

Theoretically any thing which is used to distinguish one trader's products or services from those of another trader, may be the subject of trade-mark claims.

A trade-mark may be any form of indication or sign, such as:

(a) a word (*e.g.*, "IBM", "XEROX", "EXXON");

(b) a phrase or slogan (*e.g.*, "Mr. Christie You Make Good Cookies"; "Don't Leave Home without It");[32]

(c) a logo or design (*e.g.*, the McDonald's double arches, the feather quill used by the publisher on this book);[33] or

(d) a distinctive shape (*i.e.*, the unique shape of the traditional Coca Cola bottle, the Haig & Haig "pinch" bottle, the Perrier bottle).[34]

---

[28] Fundamental to trade-mark law is use of the trade-mark. If the owner does not use the trade-mark as registered for a substantial time (generally more than three years) without a reasonable excuse then the registration of the trade-mark may be expunged for lack of use. See s. 45 (T-MA).

[29] The *Trade-marks Act* has no express limitation period. As a result, the applicable limitation period under provincial law or under the Federal Court procedure may apply. See Vaver, "Limitations in Intellectual Property: The Time is Out of Joint" (1994), 73 Can. Bar Rev. 451 for a discussion of these issues.

[30] See s. 11.19 (T-MA).

[31] See s. 53.2 (T-MA), which provides remedies by way of injunction, damages, accounts or delivery up.

[32] Trade-marks which are words or slogans are also sometimes known as "word marks".

[33] Trade-marks which are logos or designs are also sometimes known as "design marks". Such trade-marks are also likely to be protected as copyright-protected works. See Section 8, "Special Rules", *infra*.

[34] Trade-marks which are a unique shape are also known as "distinguishing guises". Note that a distinguishing guise may also be a work protectable under copyright or more likely industrial design law. See Section 8, "Special Rules", *infra*.

In addition, certain trade-marks used to designate meeting a specific standard (*e.g.*, of quality), may be registered as certification marks. Examples include the "virgin wool" logo or "CSA" (of the Canadian Standards Association).

Governments, universities, "public authorities" and certain Canadian institutions[35] may designate marks which then become prohibited for any use (whether or not a trade-mark use) in Canada. Some jurisdictions also provide protection for other indicators such as a specific sound or smell associated with a product or service.

5. Formal Requirements for Registration

The formal requirements to obtain registration of a trade-mark involve the steps of an application being filed, an internal review of the application and an external review of the application.[36] Each of these steps is briefly described below.

(a) Internal Review

The application for registration of a trade-mark is reviewed by an examiner of the Trade-marks Office. The examiner searches in the field applicable to the trade-mark being applied for and reviews the application for registrability and compliance with trade-mark law and practice. In order to be registrable the trade-mark must meet certain requirements as follows.

(i) Names or Surnames

A trade-mark is not registrable if it is primarily merely a name or surname.[37] A basic principle is that one may use one's own name as a trade-name.[38] The prohibition on registration of name or surnames is applied in a two-step test. The first step is determining whether or not the trade-mark is a name or surname.[39] The second step is to enquire, having regard to how the general Canadian public would respond, whether the trade-mark is primarily

---

[35]   A public authority is an entity which serves some broad social purpose and which has some degree of governmental control or input. See *Canadian Olympic Assn. v. Allied Corp.* (1989), 26 C.I.P.R. 157 (Fed. C.A.). Widespread use of this provision for common terms and the breadth of protection available for such marks has cast some doubt about the continued legitimacy of these special provisions under the *Trade-marks Act*.

[36]   Details on making a trade-mark application may be found in White, *op. cit.*, footnote 5.

[37]   See s. 12(1)(*a*) (T-MA).

[38]   See s. 19 (T-MA), which provides that the exclusive rights of the registered trade-mark owner do not prevent a person from using his or her own name as a trade-name. Such use must be *bona fide* (*e.g.*, you cannot change your name so as to be able to use a registered trade-mark).

[39]   The Trade-marks Office may review if the trade-mark can be found in a telephone directory.

associated with a name or surname or as a brand or associated with a business.[40]

Note that a trade-mark that is not registrable by virtue of this prohibition may be registrable if it has been so used in Canada that it has become distinctive as at the date of application for registration of that trade-mark.[41]

(ii) Descriptive or Deceptively Misdescriptive

A trade-mark is not registrable if it is clearly descriptive or deceptively misdescriptive – in either English or French – of the character or quality of the wares or services with which the trade-mark is associated.[42] A basic requirement of trade-mark law is that the trade-mark must be distinctive of the owner's wares or services.[43] Trade-mark law will not permit one trader to obtain a monopoly either on the English or French language nor on descriptive terms for wares or services. The test is one of first impression of the trade-mark by the ordinary user or dealer in the particular wares or services. The trade-mark cannot be descriptive – whether depicted, written or sounded – of the conditions of or the persons employed in the production or wares or services or the place of origin. For example, ORANGE MAISON for orange juice was not registrable.[44] Similarly, CALGARY for western apparel, GERMAN for beer, PARIS for fashion clothes would not be registrable because the trade-mark may be descriptive of the place of origin for such goods. While the trade-mark cannot be clearly descriptive it can be suggestive.

The trade-mark cannot be deceptively misdescriptive of the wares or services with which it is associated. In other words, the trade-mark cannot be misdescriptive of a character or quality of the wares or services in a manner which would mislead the public. For example, SHAMMI for a transparent polyethylene glove is not registrable since the glove did not contain any trace of chamois.[45] Note that a trade-mark can be directly misdescriptive of the

---

[40] See, for example, *Galanos v. Canada (Registrar of Trade Marks)* (1982), 69 C.P.R. (2d) 144 (Fed. T.D.). The trade-mark must have a connotation other than as a name or surname.

[41] See s. 12(2) (T-MA).

[42] See s. 12(1)(*b*) (T-MA).

[43] There are many ways in which a trade-mark may not be distinctive of the wares or services with which it is associated. One common way is if the trade-mark is descriptive of the wares or services. See, for example, *Canadian Shredded Wheat Co. v. Kellogg Co. of Canada*, [1938] 1 All E.R. 618 (P.C.): SHREDDED WHEAT was descriptive of the product.

[44] See *Home Juice Co. v. Orange Maison Ltée*, [1970] S.C.R. 942, 16 D.L.R. (3d) 740. Orange relates to the character of orange juice and maison describes a quality of the wares, namely, "home-made".

[45] See also *E. Kirstein Sons & Co. v. Cohen Bros. Ltd.* (1907), 39 S.C.R. 286 where the court found STA-ZON and SHUR-ON for eyeglass frames descriptive of the function of the frames and not registrable.

wares or services with which it would be associated. For example, EDMONTON BANANAS would not appear to be deceptively misdescriptive since no reasonable person might believe bananas might originate in Edmonton.[46]

Note that a trade-mark that is not registrable by virtue of this prohibition may be registrable if it has been so used in Canada that it has become distinctive as at the date of application for registration of that trade-mark.[47]

(iii) Name of Wares or Services

A trade-mark is not registrable if it is the name in any language of any of the wares or services with which the trade-mark is associated.[48] A basic requirement of trade-mark law is that the trade-mark must be distinctive of the owner's wares or services. Trade-mark law will not permit one trader to obtain a monopoly either on any language of the name of the wares or services. For example, SCHERE for scissors is not registrable as it is the German word for scissors.

(iv) Confusion with a Registered Trade-mark

A trade-mark is not registrable if it is confusing with any registered trade-mark.[49] For example, SMOOTHIES was found to be confusing with the prior registration for SMARTIES.[50]

(v) A Prohibited Mark

A trade-mark is not registrable if it is a mark the adoption of which is prohibited under either ss. 9 or 10 of the *Trade-marks Act.*[51] Section 9 sets out a long list of official marks.[52] Section 10 prohibits adoption of terms which are common in an industry or trade as a trade-mark. Plant denominations are also prohibited marks.[53]

---

[46]   Of course there may be objection to the "bananas" portion of the trade-mark as being descriptive of the wares.

[47]   See s. 12(2) (T-MA).

[48]   See s. 12(1)(c) (T-MA).

[49]   See s. 12(1)(d) (T-MA). See also Chapter 8, Section 2, "Scope of Rights — Confusion", *infra*, describing the factors considered and test for confusion.

[50]   See *Rowntree Co. v. Paulin Chambers Co.*, [1968] S.C.R. 134, 54 C.P.R. 43.

[51]   See s. 12(1)(c) (T-MA).

[52]   For example it provides for protection of the official marks and coats of arms of the Government of Canada or any province, the Royal Family, the Royal Canadian Mounted Police, the Red Cross, Red Cresent, Red Lion and marks of the United Nations. In addition, so-called "public authority" marks are also protected. See footnote 35, *supra*.

[53]   See *Plant Breeders' Rights Act*, S.C. 1990, c. 20, ss. 14(6), 15 and s. 11.1 (T-MA).

(b) External Review

Once the trade-mark application appears to be registrable to the examiner, it is published in the weekly Trade-marks Journal. Any interested party who feels the applicant should not be permitted to obtain registration of the applicable trade-mark may seek to oppose the trade-mark application and must do so within two months of the date of publication of the applicable Trade-marks Journal.

Trade-mark opposition proceedings are an adversarial process carried out before the Trade-marks Opposition Board.[54] There, the opponent files a statement of opposition setting out the basis of its objections to the trade-mark application. The applicant responds by filing a counter statement setting out the basis on which the applicant believes it is entitled to obtain registration. Parties file evidence in support of their positions by affidavit or other sworn document and ultimately argue their positions in front of the Trade-marks Opposition Board.

If no one has sought to oppose the trade-mark application within two months of the date of publication of the applicable Trade-marks Journal, or if opposition proceedings have concluded in favour of the applicant, the trade-mark application is normally allowed. The registration of the trade-mark would normally occur within a few months after satisfying any last substantive requirements.[55]

6. Term of Protection

The trade-mark registration subsists for fifteen years and is indefinitely renewable thereafter for additional terms of fifteen years provided the trade-mark is still being used.[56]

7. Ownership of the Rights

The entitlement to the adoption and use of a trade-mark in Canada is based on the first to either use the trade-mark in Canada, make the trade-mark known in Canada, or if neither of the above has occurred, the first to file a trade-mark application for the trade-mark in Canada. Each of these bases of entitlement are described in more detail below.

---

[54]   See s. 38 (T-MA), for factors which may be a basis for opposing an application for registration of a trade-mark.

[55]   An example of further substantive requirements might include: if the application was filed on the basis of proposed use, the trade-mark must actually be used before it may be registered. The applicant would have to file a declaration of use in this regard.

[56]   See s. 46(1) (T-MA).

(a) First Use

The person who first uses the trade-mark in commerce has the entitlement to adopt and register the trade-mark in Canada. The use must be in Canada. Recall that "use" for trade-marks purposes means

(a) in relation to products, the placement of the trade-mark on the product or on packaging for the product at the point of sale or when possession is passed to the customer of the product,[57] or

(b) in relation to services, the use of the trade-mark incidental to the provision of the services or use in advertising the ability to provide the services.[58]

To qualify, use must be real use in the ordinary course of business, not a single transaction between non-arms length parties. The use must also be in Canada. Earlier use in another jurisdiction is not use in Canada.

(b) Making Known

If the activity is not actual use in Canada there may, nonetheless, be sufficient activity in association with the trade-mark that it becomes known in Canada. In *Motel 6 Inc. v. No. 6 Motel Ltd.*,[59] the American-based operator of a chain of hotels sought to address use of a similar trade-mark by an unrelated group in Canada. The American hotel did not have a business presence in Canada and was found not to be using its trade-mark in Canada.[60]

(c) Filing an Application

If there is neither actual use in Canada nor sufficient activity in association with the trade-mark that it becomes known in Canada, then the first to file an application for the trade-mark in respect of specific products and/or services will be the person entitled to the trade-mark in respect of the applicable products and/or services in Canada.

It is important to note that under the Paris Convention[61] a foreign application claiming rights under the Convention may be filed in Canada up

---

[57]   Subsection 4(1) (T-MA).

[58]   Subsection 4(2) (T-MA).

[59]   [1982] 1 F.C. 638 (T.D.).

[60]   Note that while the Court did not find sufficient activity to be a basis for trade-mark entitlement by making the trade-mark known in Canada, nonetheless the Court did find sufficient activity in relation to the American hotel's trade-mark so that the Canadian hotel's trade-mark application for a similar trade-mark was invalid. The Canadian hotel was not the person entitled to the similar trade-mark since it was confused in the relevant marketplace with the American hotel's trade-mark.

[61]   For more information on the use and operation under the Paris Convention, see Chapter 14, "International Treaties".

to six months after it was filed in the member country of the Convention and still claim the original filing date in the foreign country as its filing date in Canada. In effect, this permits the applicant to backdate the application filed in Canada to the earlier filing date.

In addition to the rights in the trade-mark, there may also be copyrights and moral rights in a logo created to be used as a trade-mark (see Section 8(a), "Special Rules — Copyright and Trade-marks", *infra*). All applicable parties should specifically address their respective interests in any trade-mark to avoid any issues or conflict.

8. Special Rules

(a) Copyright and Trade-marks

Unlike the complications of the relationship between copyright and industrial design law or the lesser complications of copyright and patent law, the provisions of Canada's copyright law and trade-mark law coexist and complement each other in a useful manner. Unlike a trade-mark which only provides protection in relation to specific uses, copyright provides protection in relation to any substantially similar copy regardless of use.

Many traders use artistic works, such as designs, logos or distinguishing guises, as design marks to distinguish their wares and services from those of others. Such artistic works may be protected under copyright law. As a result, it may be possible for the trade-mark owner to take action respecting infringement or other unfair competition by bringing both trade-mark infringement action and copyright infringement action.

As far as possible, the trade-mark agent or advisor carrying out the registration of the trade-marks should seek to address the issue of protection of the copyright in design marks.[62]

(b) Industrial Design and Trade-marks

In some cases, distinctive shapes which may be considered for trade-mark protection as distinguishing guises may also qualify for protection under the industrial design system. In such a case, the owner should consider seeking to obtain, if still possible, industrial design protection for the unique design. Note that there is only one year from making the design or shape public in which to seek industrial design protection.

As far as possible the trade-mark agent or advisor carrying out the registration of the trade-marks should seek to address the issue of protection of any industrial design rights in a distinguishing guise.[63]

---

[62] For more details on copyright issues, see *Protection of Copyright and Industrial Design*, Practice Guide (Toronto: Carswell, 1995).

[63] For more details on industrial design issues and the application process, see *ibid*.

(c) Trade-mark Notices

A trade-mark owner is prudent to properly place notices on all trade-marks used in its advertising materials. Notices warn the public of both the existence of the trade-mark and the owner's claim to that trade-mark.

(i) Own Trade-marks

A trade-mark owner should identify its ownership clearly and unambiguously. For example, in the case of unregistered trade-marks, the trade-mark owner ("A") might indicate:

(Mark)™

(Mark) is a trade-mark of A.

In the case of registered trade-marks A might indicate:

(Mark)®

(Mark) is a registered trade-mark of A.

(ii) Licensed Trade-marks

A trade-mark owner must review the terms under which he or she is licensed to use any other person's trade-marks. There may be a requirement to identify the ownership, licensed use and other aspects of a trade-mark owner's specific obligations with the licensor. A trade-mark owner's specific obligations would govern in each such case. For illustrative purposes only (and subject to any actual obligations a trade-mark owner might have), such a notice might be as follows:

(Mark)®

(Mark) is a registered trade-mark of A used under licence by B.

(iii) Unlicensed Use of Other's Trade-marks

A trade-mark owner must exercise real care in the use of any other person's trade-marks without a licence or consent to do so.

A trade-mark owner will wish to ensure that it does not use another's trade-mark for its products or services or use a confusingly similar trade-mark or trade-name in association with a trade-mark owner's products or services. Those actions may result in liability under ss. 19 and 20 of the *Trade-marks Act* respectively.

8

Protection Of Unregistered Trade-marks

1. Introduction

Trade-marks protect the goodwill and reputation associated with a product or service. There are three broad areas or systems of law providing some degree of protection of trade-marks and reputation. These areas of law protect registered trade-marks,[1] unregistered trade-marks (discussed in this chapter), and rights in personality.[2]

Trade-marks and trade-names, including unregistered trade-marks, may receive a level of protection under the common law passing off action and the provisions of s. 7 of the *Trade-marks Act*. Other remedies may be available depending on the circumstances. The passing off action should not be confused with registration of a trade-name. The trade-name registration requirement does not — of itself — create any trade-mark rights or rights as a basis for a passing off action.

---

[1] Registered trade-marks obtain a substantial degree of protection under the registration provisions of the *Trade-marks Act*. See Chapter 7, "Trade-marks", for more details of this form of protection.

[2] Rights in a person's likeness, voice, appearance, shape or other attributes of personality may obtain a degree of protection under the common law and certain provisions of privacy legislation in some provinces. See Chapter 9, "Personality Rights", for more details of this form of protection. In some cases copyright law (Chapter 2), moral rights (Chapter 3) and/or neighbouring rights (Chapter 4) may also play a role in protecting rights in a person's likeness, voice or other attributes of the person's personality.

2. Scope of Rights

Trade-marks may be registered under the provisions of the *Trade-marks Act*.[3] An unregistered trade-mark provides the owner with certain rights to use the trade-mark in association with the products or services with which it has become known.

A trader has a right to be free of use of another trade-mark in a manner which is confusing with the trader's trade-mark or business.

(a) Common Law Passing Off Action

There exists a common law action to prevent one trader from representing its goods and services as those of another. The common law tort of passing off requires that a misrepresentation occurs which causes confusion or a risk of confusion as to an association or connection between traders.[4]

(i) *Reputation in the Market*

In order for rights to exist, the trader must have a distinctive reputation in the marketplace. The test is: Would the ordinary customer or unwary purchaser recognize a distinctive reputation?[5] Some of the factors are the inherent distinctiveness of the trade-name or unregistered trade-mark.[6] Traders who adopt common or descriptive terms under which to carry on business will be less likely to satisfy this requirement.

(ii) *Misrepresentation*

There must be a misrepresentation by the defendant to a prospective or actual customer of goods or services supplied by the plaintiff. The misrepresentation can take a variety of forms, such as, similar markings on goods, concurrent sale of goods, confusion as to the origin of goods,[7] similar business names or a confusing "get-up".[8] The test is whether customers think or might be led to think that there is a connection between the wares, services or business of the plaintiff and the defendant.[9]

---

[3]   Details on making a trade-mark application may be found in White, *Selection and Protecting Trade-marks*, Canada Practice Guide (Toronto: Carswell, 1994).

[4]   *Walt Disney Productions v. Triple Five Corp.* (1994), 53 C.P.R. (3d) 129 (Alta. C.A.).

[5]   See *Oxford Pendaflex Canada Ltd. v. Korr Marketing Ltd.*, [1982] 1 S.C.R. 494.

[6]   See s. 6(5) (T-MA) for factors which may also be applicable. Similar factual issues would be considered in a statutory or common law action.

[7]   See, for example, *Hunters Sport Shop Ltd. v. Hunter's R.V. Sales Ltd.* (1986), 13 C.P.R. (3d) 444 (Alta. Q.B.).

[8]   *Oxford Pendaflex Canada Ltd. v. Korr Marketing Ltd.*, *supra*, footnote 5.

[9]   *Walt Disney Productions v. Triple Five Corp.*, *supra*, footnote 4.

(iii) **Intention to Deceive**

The lack of an intention to deceive is irrelevant where the representation is factually false. After warning the defendant of the plaintiff's rights, some courts find that continued use may raise an inference of fraud.

The common law passing off action may not be a satisfactory remedy since it requires a common field of activity between the plaintiff and defendant. This has been an issue in many cases involving efforts to protect a well-known individual's personality.[10] The strict requirement of a common field of activity under the common law passing off action has been moderated in two ways. Firstly, some courts have extended the traditional common law passing off action to apply to such false association cases. Second, some courts have developed a new tort, misappropriation of personality (see Chapter 9, "Personality Rights").

(b) The Extended Passing Off Action

Some Canadian courts have found passing off to exist where the defendant misrepresents some association between the plaintiff and defendant even where the fields of the plaintiff's and defendant's business are quite different.[11] For example, in *National Hockey League v. Pepsi-Cola Canada Ltd.*,[12] the Court stated that there are two types of passing off. The traditional passing off action involves competitors in a common field of activity where the plaintiff alleges that the defendant has named, packaged or described its product or business in a manner likely to lead the public to believe the defendant's product or business is that of the plaintiff.[13] The other form of passing off is where it is alleged that a defendant has promoted its product or business in such a way as to create a false impression that the product or business is in some way approved, authorized or endorsed by the plaintiff or that there is a business connection between the plaintiff and defendant. By these means a defendant may hope to benefit from the goodwill of the plaintiff.[14]

As in the case of a traditional passing off action there must be a misrepresentation. There is a requirement that the "taking" of another's reputation or goodwill "must be through the medium of a misrepresentation that causes public deception and confusion as to an association between the

---

[10]   See Chapter 8, "Personality Rights".

[11]   *Seiko Time Canada Ltd. v. Consumers Distributing Co.* (1980), 29 O.R. (2d) 221 (H.C.), affd (1981), 34 O.R. (2d) 481 (C.A.), revd on other grounds (1984), 3 C.I.P.R. 223, 1 C.P.R. (3d) 1 (S.C.C.).

[12]   (1992), 42 C.P.R. (3d) 390 (B.C. S.C.).

[13]   *Supra*, at p. 401.

[14]   *Supra*.

parties. If there is no foreseeable likelihood of the public being deceived or confused, then there is no basis for recovery."[15]

(c) Statutory Action

Section 7 of the *Trade-marks Act* provides a code of statutory rules related to this subject:

7. No person shall

(*a*)   make a false or misleading statement tending to discredit the business, wares or services of a competitor;

(*b*)   direct public attention to his wares, services or business in such a way as to cause or be likely to cause confusion in Canada, at the time he commenced so to direct attention to them, between his wares, services or business and the wares, services or business of another;[16]

(*c*)   pass off other wares or services as and for those ordered or requested;

(*d*)   make use, in association with wares or services, of any description that is false in a material respect and likely to mislead the public as to

(i)   the character, quality, quantity or composition,

(ii)   the geographical origin, or

(iii) the mode of the manufacture, production or performance

of the wares or services; or

(*e*)   do any other act or adopt any other business practice contrary to honest industrial or commercial usage in Canada.[17]

As a result, it is important for a trader to ensure that it does not pass off its wares and services as somehow connected or associated with that of a competitor or that a competitor's goods or services are somehow associated with the trader. A trader must avoid any representation that its service or

---

[15]   R.G. Howell, "Character Merchandising: The Marketing Potential Attaching to a Name, Image, Persona or Copyright Work" (1991), 6 I.P.J. 197.

[16]   In *Westfair Foods Ltd. v. Jim Pattison Industries Ltd.* (1990), 30 C.P.R. (3d) 174 (B.C. C.A.), the Court referred to the rights under s. 7(*b*) as nothing more than a statutory statement of the common law tort of passing off. The constitutional validity of this section has been doubted in a number of cases but the decision of the Federal Court of Appeal in *Asbjorn Horgard A/S v. Gibbs/Nortac Industries Ltd.* (1987), 14 C.P.R. (3d) 314 (Fed. C.A.), found s. 7(*b*) to be valid.

[17]   In *MacDonald v. Vapor Canada Ltd.* (1976), 22 C.P.R. (2d) 1 (S.C.C.), the Court held that s. 7(*e*) was outside the constitutional competence of the federal government. The constitutional validity of all of s. 7 was, however, supported in the decision of the Federal Court of Appeal in *Asbjorn Horgard A/S v. Gibbs/Nortac Industries Ltd.*, *supra*, footnote 16.

product is approved, associated or otherwise connected with a competitor's product or service.

A trader will also wish to be cautious regarding the violation of the other provisions of s. 7. Note that an action under s. 7 must be brought into the Federal Court. This may limit the ability to combine the action with torts or other actions which could be brought in a provincial court of superior jurisdiction (*e.g.*, Ontario High Court or Alberta Court of Queen's Bench).

3. Limits on Enforcing Rights

Some substantial defences or limits on the enforceability of an unregistered trade-mark or trade-name include:

(a) the extent to which the plaintiff can prove that he or she has a distinctive reputation in the trade-name, trade-mark or business in the specific geographic region in which the defendant is operating.

(b) the extent to which there is a misrepresentation suggesting a connection between the trade-names, trade-marks or business of the parties.

(c) the extent to which the trade-names or trade-marks are confusing and whether or not there is evidence of actual confusion.[18]

An action for passing off may be brought in either the Federal Court (if cloaked within s. 7) or in a provincial court of superior jurisdiction.

4. Types of Things Protected

Theoretically any thing which is used to distinguish one trader's products or services from those of another trader, may be the subject of a passing off action. Examples might include a trade-mark, a trade-name or business name, a logo, the shape or appearance of a product or the trade dress of a product.[19]

5. Formal Requirements for Protection

There are no formal requirements to create the rights to bring action in respect of an unregistered trade-mark. Obviously, registration of the trade-mark would provide substantial rights.[20] The plaintiff will require a distinctive reputation in its own name or trade-mark in the region or area in which the complained-of actions occurred.

---

[18]   See Chapter 7 and the discussion of confusion and the factors set out in s. 6(5) (T-MA).

[19]   In *Eli Lilly & Co. v. Novopharm Ltd.*, [1996] F.C.J. No. 480 (Fed. T.D.), the Court granted an interlocutory injunction in a passing off case involving the proposed sale of fluoxetine hydrochloride by the defendants in a form with a size, shape and colour quite similar to that used by Lilly for its Prozac brand fluoxetine hydrochloride pharmaceutical.

[20]   See Chapter 7, "Trade-marks".

6. Term of Protection

The rights to bring an action in respect of an unregistered trade-mark are the existence of a distinctive reputation in the plaintiff's own name or trade-mark in the region or area in which the defendant's actions are complained of.

7. Ownership of the Rights

The entitlement to bring a passing off action in Canada is based on the use of the trade-mark and whether the plaintiff has a distinctive reputation in its own name or trade-mark in the region or area in which the defendant's actions are complained of. Because of the advantages of registration (including availability of exclusive rights throughout Canada) many businesses choose to supplement their common law rights by registration of the trade-mark.

8. Special Rules

In addition to the rights in the common law (unregistered) trade-mark, there may also be copyrights and moral rights in a logo or design created for use as a trade-mark. These rights may supplement or complement to trader's rights in its unregistered trade-mark.

9

Personality Rights

1. Introduction

The protection of rights in personality is one of three broad areas of law providing protection for trade-marks and reputation. As discussed in previous chapters, the other two areas protect registered trade-marks and unregistered trade-marks.[1]

Rights in one's personality or expressions of that personality are not well-developed in Canadian law.[2] Certain protection may be found under the specialized tort of appropriation of personality, some specialized provisions of the *Trade-marks Act*[3] or provisions of certain provincial legislation.[4] Other remedies may be available depending on the circumstances.[5]

2. Scope of Rights

Trade-marks may be registered under the provisions of the *Trade-marks Act*.[6] Celebrities often seek to utilize the remedies and benefits available for

---

[1] Unregistered trade-marks may obtain a degree of protection under the common law passing off action and s. 7 of the *Trade-marks Act*. See Chapter 8, "Protection of Unregistered Trade-marks", for more details of this form of protection.

[2] Contrast the more developed law providing a broad range of protection of personality and related rights in certain American states, such as, New York, NY Civ. Rights, ss. 50, 51; California, Cal. Civ. C., ss. 990 and 344; Kentucky, Ky R.S., ss. 391.170, and Nebraska, Neb. R.S.A., ss. 20-202.

[3] Details on making a trade-mark application may be found in White, *Selection and Protecting Trade-marks*, Canada Practice Guide (Toronto: Carswell, 1994).

[4] See, for example, the rights available under British Columbia's *Privacy Act*, R.S.B.C. 1996, c. 373.

[5] Depending on the facts, there may be actions under copyright law (see Chapter 2), moral rights (see Chapter 3), performers' rights (see Chapter 4) or rights in confidential information (see Chapter 11).

[6] Details on making a trade-mark application may be found in White, *op. cit.*, footnote 3.

registered trade-marks to protect certain aspects or features of their personality. Registration of a celebrity's name, however, is not without complications.[7]

The common law passing off action may not be a satisfactory remedy since it requires a common field of activity between the plaintiff and defendant.[8] In the case of *Krouse v. Chrysler Canada Ltd.*,[9] an automobile manufacturer had developed and distributed a promotional device on which it placed an action photograph of a football game. This device promoted the sale of Chrysler cars. Krouse, a professional football player, was clearly identifiable in the photograph. The action based on passing off failed, since no one would be confused and believe that Krouse was manufacturing or selling cars.

This strict – and some argue narrow – approach available under the common law passing off action has been moderated in two ways. Firstly, some courts have extended the traditional common law passing off action to apply to such false association cases.[10] Second, some courts have developed a new tort, misappropriation of personality.

(a) The Extended Passing Off Action

The extended passing off action may provide a remedy where it is alleged that a defendant has promoted a product or business in such a way as to create a false impression that his product or business is in some way approved, authorized or endorsed by the plaintiff or that there is a business connection between the plaintiff and defendant. By these means a defendant may hope to "cash in" on the goodwill of the plaintiff.[11] As in the case of a traditional passing off action, there must be a misrepresentation. There is a requirement that the "taking" of another's reputation or goodwill "must be through the medium of a misrepresentation that causes public deception and confusion as to an association between the parties. If there is no foreseeable likelihood of the public being deceived or confused, then there is no basis for recovery."[12]

---

[7]   See Chapter 7, "Trade-marks", dealing with the requirements for registrability of a trade-mark. Words that are primarily merely names or surnames are not registrable: s. 12 (T-MA).

[8]   See Chapter 8, "Protection of Unregistered Trade-marks".

[9]   (1974), 1 O.R. (2d) 225 (C.A.).

[10]   See the discussion of the "extended action" in Section 2(b) of Chapter 8.

[11]   See, for example, *National Hockey League v. Pepsi-Cola Canada Ltd.* (1992), 42 C.P.R. (3d) 390 at 401 (B.C. S.C.), additional reasons at (1993), 48 C.P.R. (3d) 149 (B.C. S.C.).

[12]   R.G. Howell, "Character Merchandising: The Marketing Potential Attaching to a Name, Image, Persona or Copyright Work" (1991), 6 I.P.J. 197 at 203.

(b) Misappropriation of Personality Action

Some courts[13] in Canada have developed a tort of misappropriation of personality. The key to this action is the wrongful use for commercial gain of another's name, voice, likeness or other aspect of personality. There may be an issue whether or not this tort exists in provinces which have enacted statutory protection of privacy giving an individual a right of action in such circumstances.[14]

In *Krouse v. Chrysler Canada Ltd.*,[15] while the Court found no traditional passing off since there was no common field of activity, the Court did go on to find that there may be circumstances in which the Courts would be justified in finding a defendant liable in damages for appropriation of a plaintiff's personality, amounting to an invasion of the plaintiff's right to exploit his or her personality by the use of the plaintiff's image, voice or otherwise. In the facts of that case, the Court found that there was no such misappropriation. The Court noted that professional athletes are public figures and the photograph showing Krouse was not used in a way to cause the public to think that Krouse was endorsing the defendant's cars.

In a later case, *Athans v. Canadian Adventure Camps Ltd.*,[16] the Court reaffirmed the requirement of a commercial use in this action. In this case Athans was a famous water skier. A summer camp used a distinctive photograph of Athans in a promotional brochure. The Court found the defendant's brochure had not established a connection in the mind of the public between Athans and the summer camp and in consequence found no wrongful appropriation of personality. Later cases have recognized this tort.[17]

This tort is still being developed and it can be expected that future cases will serve to flesh out more details of the action. Professor Howell, a leading scholar in this field, suggests that the requirements of the action be that there be a wrongful appropriation of personality. The issue is "whether there has been a taking, conversion or usurpation of the celebrity's identity to such an extent that the usurper should be held culpable."[18]

---

[13]   Largely cases have been from the Ontario and British Columbia courts.

[14]   In British Columbia, for example, s. 3 of the *Privacy Act*, R.S.B.C. 1979, c. 336 arguably addresses such a misappropriation of personality: See D. Vaver, "Commercial Appropriation of Personality Under the Privacy Acts of British Columbia, Manitoba and Saskatchewan" (1981), 15 U.B.C. L. Rev. 241; R.W. Judge, "Celebrity Look-Alikes and Sound-Alikes or Imitation is Not the Highest Form of Flattery" (1988), 20 C.P.R. (3d) 97.

[15]   *Supra*, footnote 9.

[16]   (1977), 80 D.L.R. (3d) 583, 17 O.R. (2d) 425 (H.C.).

[17]   See, for example, *Baron Philippe de Rothschild S.A. v. Casa de Habana Inc.* (1987), 17 C.I.P.R. 185, 19 C.P.R. (3d) 114 (Ont. H.C.); *Joseph v. Daniels* (1986), 11 C.P.R. (3d) 544, 4 B.C.L.R. (2d) 239 (S.C.); *Dowell v. Mengen Institution* (1983), 72 C.P.R. (2d) 238 (Ont. H.C.), and cases cited therein.

[18]   R.G. Howell, *op. cit.*, footnote 12, at p. 208.

(c) Trade-marks Act

Paragraph 9(1)(*k*) of the *Trade-marks Act* provides that "[n]o person shall adopt in connection with a business, as a trade-mark or otherwise, any mark consisting of, or so nearly resembling as to be likely to be mistaken for, any matter that may falsely suggest a connection with any living individual". In *Baron Philippe de Rothschild S.A. v. Casa de Habana Inc.*,[19] this section was applied when a cigar vendor sought to rely on the prestige of the Rothschild name without authorization.

As noted above, substantial remedies may be available under trade-mark law if the celebrity registers his or her distinctive nickname, team number or other element.

(d) Privacy Legislation

Certain provinces have enacted privacy legislation including a private cause of action of misuse of personality.[20] British Columbia's *Privacy Act*, R.S.B.C. 1996, c. 373, has received the greatest judicial review and will be used to illustrate some of the elements of such legislation.[21]

Section 3 of British Columbia's *Privacy Act* provides that "it is a tort, actionable without proof of damage, for a person to use the name or portrait of another for the purpose of advertising or promoting the sale of, or other trading in, property or services unless that other, or a person entitled to consent on his behalf, consents to the use for that purpose".[22]

3. Limits on a Misappropriation of Personality Action

Some substantial defences or limits on the enforceability of rights in a personality are:

(a) the extent to which the plaintiff can prove that he or she has a distinctive reputation in his or her personality.

(b) the extent to which there is wrongful use for commercial gain of another's name, voice, likeness or other aspect of personality.

The action for misappropriation of personality would be brought in a provincial court of superior jurisdiction.

---

[19]   *Supra*, footnote 17.

[20]   For commentary on these legislative provisions, see Vaver, *op. cit.*, footnote 14 and Judge, *op. cit.*, footnote 14.

[21]   See also the Privacy Acts of Manitoba, *Privacy Act*, S.M. 1970, c. 74; Saskatchewan, *Privacy Act*, R.S.S. 1978, c. P-28; and Newfoundland, *Privacy Act*, S.N. 1981, c. 6.

[22]   Subsection 3(5) of British Columbia's *Privacy Act* defines "portrait" as meaning a likeness, still or moving, and includes a likeness of another deliberately disguised to resemble the plaintiff, and a caricature.

4. Types of Things Protected

Theoretically this tort may be available to protect one's name, voice, likeness or other aspect of personality.

5. Formal Requirements for Protection

There are no formal requirements to create the rights to bring action for misappropriation of one's personality. The plaintiff will require a distinctive reputation in name, voice, likeness or other aspect of personality. The celebrity may wish to supplement this tort with the rights available by registration of applicable trade-marks.

6. Term of Protection

The rights to bring a misappropriation of personality action coexist with a distinctive reputation in the name, voice, likeness or other aspect of personality.

7. Ownership of the Rights

The entitlement to bring a misappropriation of personality action in Canada is based on the existence and use of a distinctive reputation in the name, voice, likeness or other aspect of personality.

8. Special Rules

Depending on the facts, there may be rights under copyright law (see Chapter 2), moral rights (see Chapter 3), performers' rights (see Chapter 4) or rights in confidential information (see Chapter 11) which may coexist and enhance rights in one's personality, name, voice, image and likeness.

10

Plant Breeders' Rights

1. Introduction

Considerable creativity and effort is involved in the creation of new plant varieties. Patent law may not be available to provide protection for new crop varieties arising from selective cross-breeding.[1] The *Plant Breeders' Rights Act*, S.C. 1990, c. 20, ss. 1-78,[2] provides a system for legal protection of new crop varieties. Under this system the breeder of a distinct plant variety may obtain a limited monopoly over the production and sale of the reproductive material (*i.e.*, seeds). The breeder may also be able to denominate (*i.e.*, name) the new crop variety.

2. Scope of Rights

Plant breeders' rights may be described as the following exclusive rights:

(a) a sales right;

(b) a propagation right;

(c) for plants used as ornamental flowers, a right to use and cut flowers; and

(d) a right to denominate the new plant variety.

---

[1] See *Pioneer Hi-Bred Ltd. v. Canada (Commissioner of Patents)* (1987), 14 C.P.R. (3d) 491 (Fed. C.A.), affd (1987), 25 C.I.P.R. 1, 25 C.P.R. (3d) 257 (S.C.C.): rejecting patent protection for a new soya bean variety achieved by selective cross-breeding. In part the Court found that the disclosure requirements of patent law were not met.

[2] Note that all future footnote references to this Act will be indicated by ("PBRA") following the section number. For an electronic version of the Act, see <http://xinfo.ic.gc.ca/>.

(a) Sales Right

The owner of the plant breeder's right has the exclusive right to sell, and produce in Canada for the purpose of selling, propagating material of the plant variety.[3]

(b) Propagation Right

The owner of the plant breeder's right has the exclusive right to make repeated use of the propagating material of the plant variety in order to produce a new variety of plant, if repetition is necessary for that purpose.[4]

(c) Use Right in Relation to Ornamental Varieties

The owner of the plant breeder's right has the exclusive right, in relation to ornamental plant varieties which are normally sold or marketed for purposes other than propagation, to use any such plants or parts thereof commercially as propagating material in the production of ornamental plants or cut flowers.[5]

(d) Denomination Right

The owner of the plant breeder's right has the right to propose a denomination for the new plant variety for which an application for a grant of plant breeders' rights has been made.[6]

In addition to these exclusive rights, the owner also has the right to authorize others to carry out any of the acts contemplated by those rights either on condition or unconditionally.[7]

It is an infringement of the plant breeder's right if a person, without the consent of the owner of the plant breeder's rights, exercises any of those rights without the owner's consent.[8]

3. Limits on Plant Breeders' Rights

Some substantial defences or limits on plant breeders' rights are:

---

[3]   Paragraph 5(1)(*a*) (PBRA).

[4]   See s. 5(1)(*b*) (PBRA); See also *Pioneer Hi-Bred Ltd. v. Canada (Commissioner of Patents)*, *supra*, footnote 1: selective cross-breeding to create a new crop variety did not meet the disclosure requirements for patent protection.

[5]   See s. 5(1)(*c*) (PBRA).

[6]   See s. 14(1) (PBRA). If approved, the denomination is required to be used by each person designating that plant variety for sale of the propagating material.

[7]   See s. 5(1)(*d*) (PBRA).

[8]   See s. 41(1) (PBRA). See also s. 5(1)(*d*) which permits the owner to authorize others' actions in exercise of the plant breeder's rights.

(a) the sale right does not apply in respect of sale of propagation material that is not in Canada when it is sold and so long as it is not used as propagation material in Canada.[9]

(b) the grant of plant breeders' rights must meet all of the requirements for a grant of such rights.[10]

The full range of remedies are available for an infringement of plant breeders' rights.[11] An action for infringement of plant breeders' rights may be brought in the provincial courts of superior jurisdiction[12] or in the Federal Court.[13]

4. Types of Things Protected

Examples of potentially protected plants may be a line, clone, hybrid or genetic variation of a plant. To be registrable the new variety must be stable, uniform and distinct.

5. Formal Requirements for Protection

The patentability of higher life forms is uncertain under Canadian law.[14] In the case of a new variety of a recently prescribed category, in order to be capable of protection the new plant variety may not have been sold in Canada prior to filing of the application (and receiving the receipt for filing the application).[15] Other varieties may have been sold in Canada before the effective date of the application. The variety not have been sold for more than four years in other countries (six years for certain slow growing varieties).

The new variety must be

(a) distinct, *i.e.*, different from other existing plant varieties;

---

[9]   See s. 5(2) (PBRA).

[10]   As a result, the grant could be attacked on a failure to meet any of the requirements for a grant of these rights. See Section 4, "Types of Things Protected".

[11]   See s. 41(1) (PBRA), which provides remedies by way of damages and s. 41(2) which provides remedies by way of injunction, damages, accounts or delivery up. These are available to the owner of the plant breeder's rights.

[12]   See s. 42(1) (PBRA).

[13]   See s. 43(1) (PBRA).

[14]   See *Pioneer Hi-Bred Ltd. v. Canada (Commissioner of Patents)*, *supra*, footnote 1. There, a patent application for a new soya bean variety was found not to be patentable. The new crop variety was the result of selected cross-breeding and the Court found it did not meet the disclosure requirements under the *Patent Act*. Regrettably the Court did not use this opportunity to address the issue of patent protection of higher life forms which may otherwise satisfy the requirements of patent protection. It appears that a new crop variety created by selective cross-breeding may now be under the protection of the *Plant Breeders' Rights Act*.

[15]   See s. 7(1)(*a*) (PBRA).

(b) uniform, *i.e.*, all plants must be similar to each other; and

(c) stable, *i.e.*, next generations of the plant variety will resemble the parents.

The Act has special provisions dealing with recently prescribed categories and prescribed exemptions.[16]

The applicant must be a Canadian citizen or resident of Canada or have a registered office in Canada or a country of the Union.[17] The application must be made in the prescribed form, filed together with the applicable fee and supportive materials.[18] The applicant has the right to propose a denomination for the new plant variety.[19]

6. Term of Protection

The term of protection provided under the Act is eighteen years from the date of issue of the grant of the rights.[20]

7. Ownership of the Rights

The breeder is the person entitled to make application for the plant breeder's rights. The plant breeder's rights may be assigned by the breeder.[21] Assignments of plant breeders' rights must comply with certain formalities.[22]

8. Special Rules

Applicants for plant breeders' rights should consider whether or not the method or process of making the new plant variety or the resulting product satisfies the requirements for patentability.

---

[16]   See s. 7 (PBRA).

[17]   See s. 8 (PBRA) and the provisions of the 1978 *International Union for the Protection of New Varieties of Plants* ("UPOV") to which Canada adhered on March 4, 1991.

[18]   See s. 9(1) (PBRA).

[19]   See s. 14(1) (PBRA). If approved, the denomination is required to be used by each person designating that plant variety for sale of the propagating material.

[20]   See s. 6(1) (PBRA).

[21]   See s. 31(1) (PBRA).

[22]   See s. 31(1) (PBRA). The Commissioner must be informed of the assignment and details of the assignment within a prescribed period.

11

Trade Secrets

1. Introduction

Both technical and business information, data, ideas, plans, designs or concepts may be protected under trade secret law. Historically in England the chancellor had jurisdiction over a person's conscience and might provide relief when strict application of the common law would lead to injustice. Over time, courts of chancery were established and administered a system of discretionary remedies known as equity. Among those remedies was the binding of a person's conscience to require maintenance of secret information in confidence.[1] This action became known as the breach of confidence action.

Note that obligations of confidence may also arise under contract (in which case there may be rights under equity and rights under the contract). It has been proposed that the common law be supplemented by a statutory form of trade secret law.[2]

A key feature of an obligation of confidence is the existence of a secret.

2. Scope of Rights

The breach of confidence action gives the person to whom the obligation of confidence is owed, the right to require the person who owes the obligation to keep the information secret.[3]

---

[1]   See, for further background, *Saltman Engineering Co. v. Campbell Engineering Co.*, [1963] 3 All E.R. 413, 65 R.P.C. 203 (U.K. C.A.); and *Seager v. Copydex Ltd.*, [1967] 1 W.L.R. 923, [1967] R.P.C. 349, [1967] 2 All E.R. 415 (U.K. C.A.), and cases cited therein.

[2]   See Report No. 46 on Trade Secrets, Institute of Law Research and Reform, Alberta, for a proposed act and background discussion.

[3]   For implications to trade secrets of the internet, see Gahtan, Kratz, Mann, *Internet Law*, (Carswell, 1998).

(a) Restriction on Disclosure

The person to whom the obligation of confidence is owed has the right to require the person who owes the obligation to refrain from the disclosure of the confidential information.[4]

(b) Use Restriction Right

In many cases, the contractual or fiduciary obligations[5] may obligate the person who owes an obligation of confidence to refrain from certain uses of the confidential information. In such cases the person to whom the obligation of confidence is owed may have the right to insist that the person bound by the obligation of confidence use the confidential information only for the purposes of the owner.[6]

In addition, the owner of the confidential information also has the right to authorize others to use or disclose the confidential information.

3. Elements of the Cause of Action

The elements of the breach of confidence action include a relationship of confidence, specific confidential information and detriment arising from disclosure.

(a) A Relationship of Confidence

There must be an obligation of confidence owed in relation to the specific confidential information. There must be a relationship between the person who owns the confidential information and the person who is to be bound by the obligation of confidence. The obligation of confidence may arise from a variety of relationships, including:

---

[4]   See, for example, *International Corona Resources Ltd. v. LAC Minerals Ltd.* (1989), 44 B.L.R. 1 (S.C.C.).

[5]   An obligation of confidence arises in a fiduciary relationship. Note that the fiduciary also has other obligations owed to the party who has the benefit of the fiduciary relationship. See, for example, *Boardman v. Phipps*, [1967] 2 A.C. 46 (H.L.): where a fiduciary was prevented from making any use of the information he acquired for his own benefit.

[6]   Technically, under present Canadian law, the person to whom the obligation of confidence is owned does not appear to "own" property in the sense contemplated by the criminal law (in this chapter the person to whom the obligation of confidence is owned will be referred to as the "owner" of the trade secret): See *R. v. Stewart* (1983), 42 O.R. (2d) 225 (C.A.), revd (1988), 41 C.C.C. (3d) 481, 50 D.L.R. (4th) 1 (S.C.C.). The Court did not consider equitable obligations to be property. Presumably the same result would arise where there were contractual obligations of confidence as well.

(a) an express obligation of confidence such as in a non-disclosure agreement;[7] or

(b) implied obligations of confidence as may arise:

> i.   In circumstances where there is an obligation of confidence implied, such as during pre-contractual negotiations.[8]

> ii.   In circumstances where the obligation of confidence is implied by law, such as in a fiduciary relationship.[9]

Sometimes employees are also bound by obligations in their relationship with the employer sometimes characterized as fiduciary obligations.[10] Sometimes the courts appear to confuse the requirement for an obligation of confidence with the higher requirements of a fiduciary relationship. For example, in *International Corona Resources Ltd. v. LAC Minerals Ltd.*[11] some of the Justices found a fiduciary relationship between two mining companies in pre-contractual negotiations.

(b) Confidential Information

In order for there to be an obligation of confidence, the information must be confidential.[12] As a result any publication or disclosure of the specific information would make the information available to the public. This must be considered when making patent applications or seeking other forms of protection where the application (or if granted, the registration) is available to the public. Other examples of disclosures which would preclude protection include: publication of the information in an article or brochure, public use or sale of a product embodying the information or from which the information may be extracted.

Note that the confidential information may be knowledge of the intent of another party respecting information which is available to the public.[13]

---

[7]   See, for example, *Eli Lilly Can. Inc. v. Shamrock Chems. Ltd.*, [1986] 6 C.I.P.R. 5 (Ont. H.C.). For several examples of non-disclosure agreements, see the appendices to *Obtaining Patents*, Practice Guide (Toronto: Carswell, 1995).

[8]   See, for example, *Seager v. Copydex Ltd.*, *supra*, footnote 1; *International Corona Resources Ltd. v. LAC Minerals Ltd.*, *supra*, footnote 4. In each such case there were circumstances suggesting the existence of obligations of confidence.

[9]   See, for example, *Boardman v. Phipps*, *supra*, footnote 5.

[10]   See *Hivac Ltd. v. Park Royal Scientific Instruments Ltd.*, [1946] Ch. 169 (U.K. C.A.) and *Chevron Standard Ltd. v. Home Oil Co.* (1981), 50 C.P.R. (2d) 182 (Alta. Q.B.), affd (1982), 64 C.P.R. (2d) 11 (Alta. C.A.), leave to appeal to S.C.C. refused [1982] 2 S.C.R. vii.

[11]   *Supra*, footnote 4.

[12]   *Saltman Engineering Co. v. Campbell Engineering Co.*, *supra*, footnote 1; *Schauenburg Industries Ltd. v. Borowski* (1979), 50 C.P.R. (2d) 69 (Ont. H.C.).

[13]   *International Corona Resources Ltd. v. LAC Minerals Ltd.*, *supra*, footnote 4.

(c) Unauthorized Use or Disclosure to the Detriment of the Discloser

In order to be actionable the unauthorized use or disclosure must be to the detriment of the owner.[14] This is usually not difficult for the plaintiff to show since loss of control over the information usually is to the detriment of the owner. This can result in loss of the head start associated with knowledge and control of the information.[15]

Unauthorized use or disclosure is actionable if a person who owes an obligation of confidence discloses or misuses the confidential information or any part thereof without the consent of the owner.[16] The full range of remedies are available for violation of a breach of confidence.[17]

In the case of an innocent third party who acquires the confidential information without notice of the breach of the obligation of confidence but is subsequently informed of the breach, the third party is also bound by the obligation of confidence so long as the information is not yet published.[18]

4. Limits on the Action

The equitable nature of the breach of confidence action gives rise to unique limits on the action. Given the equitable basis of the obligation of confidence, it is critical that there be a relationship between the owner of the confidential information and the person who is to be bound by the obligation of confidence. The requirement for a relationship means that the rights involved in the protection of confidential information are only *in personam*, not *in rem*. This is a considerable limit on the protection available under trade

---

[14] *Supra.*

[15] *Chevron Standard Ltd. v. Home Oil Co.*, [1980] 5 W.W.R. 624 (Alta. Q.B.), affd (1982), 64 C.P.R. (2d) 11, 19 Alta. L.R. (2d) 1, 35 A.R. 550 (C.A.), leave to appeal to S.C.C. refused [1982] 2 S.C.R. vi.

[16] See, for example, *Coco v. A.N. Clark (Engineers) Ltd.*, [1969] R.P.C. 41 (U.K. Ch.); *Slavutych v. Baker* (1975), 55 D.L.R. (3d) 224, [1975] 4 W.W.R. 620 (S.C.C.), and *R.L. Crain Ltd. v. Ashton*, [1949] O.R. 303 (H.C.), affd (1949), [1950] O.R. 62 (C.A.).

[17] A very common form of relief is an interlocutory injunction and then permanent injunction, see *International Tools Ltd. v. Kollar* (1968), 67 D.L.R. (2d) 386 (Ont. C.A.).

Other forms of relief available include:

> (a) damages, see *Seager v. Copydex Ltd. (No. 2)*, [1969] 2 All E.R. 718 (U.K. C.A.), *Schauenburg Industries Ltd. v. Borowski* (1979), 50 C.P.R. (2d) 69 (Ont. H.C.);

> (b) an account of profits, see *Peter Pan Manufacturing Corp. v. Corsets Silhouette Ltd.*, [1963] 3 All E.R. 402 (U.K. Ch.);

> (c) a constructive trust, see *Pre-Cam Exploration & Development Ltd. v. McTavish*, [1966] S.C.R. 551, 57 D.L.R. (2d) 557, and

> (d) an order for delivery-up, see *International Corona Resources Ltd. v. LAC Minerals Ltd., supra*, footnote 4.

[18] See, for example, *Wheatly v. Bell*, [1984] F.S.R. 16 (S.C.N.S.W.).

secret law. As a result some kinds of industrial espionage activity may not be caught by this action.[19]

Other limits on this cause of action include:

(a) loss of confidence;[20]

(b) just cause or excuse;[21]

(c) disclosure required by law such as in legal proceedings or in investigation by a regulatory body,[22] securities regulation, patent applications and like applications; and

(d) any of the equitable remedies.

5. Types of Things Protected

The law providing protection for obligations of confidence provides protection for any type of information, data, business plans, technical results, trade or other secrets.

6. Formal Requirements for Protection

There are no formal requirements to create a right in confidential information. The elements of the breach of confidence action have been developed by judicial decision over a long period and provide the framework in which the obligations arise. These are discussed in Section 2, "Scope of Rights", *supra*.

The requirement of an obligation of confidence means that the disclosing party must have a relationship with the receiving party. No obligations arise with strangers. This is an important limit on the protection available under trade secret law.

7. Term of Protection

Theoretically, a trade secret or obligation of confidence can last indefinitely. Confidential information may be protected for as long as the information is maintained as secret. The key is to maintain the secret and obligations of confidence with all persons having access to the secret.

---

[19] See, for example, *Franklin v. Giddins*, [1978] Qd R. 72 (Aust. S.C.); *R. v. Stewart* (1982), 68 C.C.C. (2d) 305 (Ont. H.C.), revd (1983), 42 O.R. (2d) 225 (C.A.), revd (1988), 41 C.C.C. (3d) 481, 50 D.L.R. (4th) 1 (S.C.C.).

[20] See, for example, *Attorney–General v. Times Newspapers Ltd.*, [1973] 3 All E.R. 54, [1974] A.C. 273 (H.L.).

[21] See, for example, *Canadian Javelin Ltd. v. Sparling* (1978), 4 B.L.R. 153 (Fed. T.D.), and *Lennon v. News Group Newspapers Ltd.*, [1978] F.S.R. 573 (C.A.).

[22] See, for example, *Competition Act*, R.S.C. 1985, c. C-34; *National Energy Board Act*, R.S.C. 1985, c. N-7; *Investment Canada Act*, S.C. 1985, c. 28.

8. Ownership of the Rights

It is somewhat difficult to discuss "ownership" of a trade secret. Since the law recognizes an equitable obligation to maintain a confidence, the right (a chose in action) is "owned", but the secret itself is not property and cannot therefore be owned in the same sense as other physical property.[23] Of course the obligation will be owed to a party who benefits from the obligation of confidence.

A fiduciary (such as a director or senior officer) is precluded from obtaining for him or herself, either secretly or without the approval of the company, any property or business advantage belonging to the company or for which it has been negotiating.[24] Note that an employee cannot disclose confidential information of the employer.[25]

In commercial agreements trade secrets and confidential information are often purportedly assigned but it is the obligation of confidence owed to the owner of the secret or confidential information that is assigned or dealt with.

9. Special Rules

Copyright may co-exist with trade secret protection.[26] One should also consider rights in personality, moral rights and trade-marks in seeking to protect some aspects of human endeavour.

---

[23]   See *R. v. Stewart, supra*, footnote 19, in which the Supreme Court held that confidential information was not property for the purposes of the *Criminal Code*, R.S.C. 1985, c. C-46, theft provision and therefore could not be stolen since there was no deprivation. For a critique of this decision, see Kratz, "A Review of Canada's Computer Crime and Computer Abuse Laws" (1990), 7:12 C.C.L.R. 125 and 8:1 C.C.L.R. 1.

[24]   *Canadian Aero Service Ltd. v. O'Malley* (1973), 11 C.P.R. (2d) 206 (S.C.C.).

[25]   *Scapa Dryers (Can.) Ltd. v. Fardeau* (1971), 1 C.P.R. (2d) 199 (Que. S.C.).

[26]   See s. 89 (CA) [Note: this issue formerly dealt with in s. 63].

12

Patents

1. Introduction

Historically, a patent was a grant under royal privilege and proof of an entitlement to do something. As early as 1331, the King granted letter patent to foreigners wishing to practise a craft a safe conduct pass. Later the law recognized two types of patents:

(a) the exclusive right to practise some monopoly in an existing article (such as printing playing cards), and

(b) the exclusive rights in inventions.

Because of abuses of these privileges the Crown's prerogative right to grant patents was restricted[1] and a legitimate role for patents in relation to inventions was emphasized.

By the 1700s inventors were required to disclose the specifications of their invention. This has led to the current system which is based on the theory that the limited monopoly granted under a patent is in exchange for the disclosure of how the invention works.[2] Today patents provide the foundation of many businesses and provide substantial monopoly rights to the owner.

Patents are a statutory monopoly right granted for a specific invention. This monopoly right arises under the *Patent Act*, R.S.C. 1985, c. P-4.[3] A patent grant provides the owner with the exclusive right to use the invention, to manufacture or have others manufacture it and to sell a product incorporating it.

---

[1] See *Darcy v. Allein* (1602), 11 Co. Rep. 846.

[2] Note that this disclosure precludes protection of any information so disclosed as confidential information. See Chapter 11, "Trade Secrets", for more details.

[3] Note that all future foonote references to the *Patent Act* will be indicated by "PA" following the section number. For an electronic version of the Act, see <http://xinfo.ic.gc.ca/>.

It is important to note that the inventor or owner (if not the inventor) has no rights until and unless a patent is granted from the applicable patent office. The inventor or owner (if not the inventor) has no rights in a country unless a patent has been applied for and is issued from the applicable patent office in that country.

2. Scope of Rights

A patent provides protection for inventions. An invention is defined as "any new and useful art, process, machine, manufacture or composition of matter, or any new and useful improvement in any art, process, machine, manufacture or composition of matter".[4] Patent protection is only available in a registry system. Rights only arise on registration (issue or grant) of the application for a patent.

Unlike copyright, which only protects against copying (and certain other acts), an issued patent provides an exclusive monopoly right to make, use or sell any product or process incorporating the claimed invention in the jurisdiction.[5] That right may even be exercised against a person who independently invented a similar invention (but failed to make application for a patent before the patentee). The rights in a granted patent are separate and apart from the rights in the product which practises or incorporates the invention. For example, purchase of a patented product does not give the purchaser any rights to the patent.

An issued patent provides the owner the exclusive right in Canada to make, use, construct and sell the invention claimed in the patent.[6] These rights are described below.

(a) Use Right

The right to use involves the right to practise the advantages offered by the patented product or process. For example, the right to use an inventive brake system in your car or the right to use an inventive process to make widgets are illustrations of exercising the right to use. The patentee can authorize others to exercise these rights or any of them.

The right to use is implied on a sale authorized by the patentee. For example, if the claims describe a certain machine, on the sale of the machine by the patentee (or with his or her authority) the purchaser may freely use the machine for the purpose for which it was intended.

Unless there is an agreement to the contrary, the patentee can no longer control the use of the machine in the marketplace. The purchaser or a successor in title of the machine can freely use the machine without restriction

---

[4]   Section 2 (PA).

[5]   See s. 42 (PA).

[6]   See s. 42 (PA).

from the patentee. In such a case the right to use is implied for the rightful purchaser of the patented product or his or her successor in title.

(b) Right to Manufacture

The right to manufacture involves the right to make or have made by others the patented product and in some cases to repair the patented products. The patentee can authorize others to exercise these rights or any of them.

The right to make or authorize someone to make the invention is not exhausted after an authorized sale by the patentee. For example, if the claims describe a certain product, after the manufacture and sale of the product by the patentee (or with his or her authority), the patentee may still control the manufacture of other products and in some cases repair of the specific product. The purchaser of the product cannot manufacture additional products without consent of the patentee.

(c) Right to Sell

The right to sell involves the right to sell or have others sell the patented product or process. The patentee can authorize others to exercise these rights.

The right to sell is exhausted after the first sale authorized by the patentee. For example, if the claims describe a certain machine, after the sale of the machine by the patentee (or with his or her authority) the patentee can no longer control subsequent sales of the machine in the marketplace. The purchaser of the machine can freely resell the machine without restriction from the patentee.

3. Limits on Patent Rights

Some substantial defences or limits on the enforceability of a valid and subsisting patent are:

(a) any defect in registration;[7]

(b) any prior publication or making known of the invention before the patent application is filed in the applicable country;[8]

---

[7] See Section 5, "Formal Requirements for Protection", *infra*, which describes the requirements for application for a patent in Canada. See also s. 53 (PA).

[8] See the discussion of the requirements of novelty in Section 4, "Types of Things Protected", *infra*. In summary, to maximize the ability to make a valid patent application

    (a) anywhere in the world, no disclosure of the invention should be carried out anywhere;

    (b) in the United States and Canada, no disclosure of the invention should be carried out anywhere and no description of the invention published in a printed publication anywhere in either case more than one year before the application is filed in the United States Patent and Trade-mark Office and the Canadian Patent Office; or

(c) any use of the ideas or concepts not described in the claims of the patent;[9]

(d) any use of the patent after it has expired;[10]

(e) abuse of the patent rights by the owner;[11]

(f) certain limited and specialized uses;[12]

(g) certain prior sales[13] or prior use,[14] and

(h) limitations of actions.[15]

If the invention is an improvement over something that existed before (such as a process, machine, product or composition of matter), the rights of the patentee do not extend to the prior thing (the prior process, machine,

---

(c) in the United States, only no disclosure of the invention should be carried out in the United States and no description of the invention published in a printed publication anywhere in either case more than one year before the application is filed in the United States Patent and Trade-mark Office.

[9] A patent protects only the physical embodiment of the inventive idea or concepts as defined by the claims, not the idea or concepts themselves.

[10] The statutory monopoly is for a specific period of time (in Canada twenty years from date of application). Once that time has ended the exclusive rights are also ended.

[11] Certain misuse of patent rights may give rise to action under s. 66 (PA); or ss. 32, 61(1), 79(5) of the *Competition Act*. Remedies include grant of compulsory licences, limits on the patent rights and otherwise. The sale of patented medicines or foods at prices considered excessive may give rise to review by the Patented Medicine Prices Review Board and liability under ss. 79-103 (PA).

[12] Section 23 (PA), provides that a patent will not "extend to prevent the use of any invention in any ship, vessel, aircraft or land vehicle of any country entering Canada temporarily or accidentally". This provision applies so long as the invention is used solely for the needs of the ship, vessel, aircraft or land vehicle and is not used to manufacture goods to be sold in Canada or to be exported from Canada. For an exemption in respect of certain uses for national defence purposes, see s. 19 (PA).

[13] Subsection 55.2(1) specifies that it is not an infringement of a patent to make, use or sell the patented invention solely for purposes reasonably related to the development or submission of information required under any law in Canada, or of a province, that regulates the manufacture, construction, use or sale of a product. Subsection 55.2(2) specifies that in cases in which s. 55.2(1) applies that it is not an infringement to make, construct or use the invention, during any period provided by regulation, for the manufacture and storage of article intended for sale after the term of the patent expires. Subsection 56(1) (PA), provides that a person who, before the claim date in a patent, "purchased, constructed or acquired the specific article, machine, manufacture or composition of matter patented" has the right to use and sell to others the invention in respect of the said specific article, machine, manufacture or composition of matter.

[14] See *Lido Industrial Products Ltd. v. Teledyne Industries Inc.* (1981), 57 C.P.R. (2d) 29 (Fed. C.A.), leave to appeal to S.C.C. refused (1981), 59 C.P.R. (2d) 183 (S.C.C.).

[15] See *Invacare Corp. v. Everest & Jennings Canada Ltd.* (1987), 14 C.P.R. (3d) 156 (Fed. T.D.). See also s. 55.01 (PA).

product or composition of matter). In such a case the patentee may be infringing on the rights of third parties in the prior thing.[16] For example, if one patented an improvement to a machine, then one may own rights to the improvement patent but one would *not* have a right to use, manufacture or sell the machine (if the machine design itself was protected by patent) without the consent of the patentee of the machine patent. Similarly, the owner of the first machine patent would *not* have a right to use, manufacture or sell the improvement claimed by the later patent.

Infringing activity requires proof by the plaintiff that, without the consent of the owner of a patent, a defendant made, used or sold, without lawful authority or defence, a product or process (as applicable) coming within the claims of the plaintiff's valid unexpired patent. The test for determining infringement is whether or not the defendant's conduct comes within either or both the literal meaning of the claims or the pith and substance of the claims.[17]

A defendant may be liable for commiting the infringing acts or for inducing the infringement.[18] Ownership of a patent gives the owner the exclusive rights to practise the invention.[19] The full range of remedies are available for an infringement of the patent rights.[20] The patent owner has certain rights to restrict importation of infringing goods.[21]

The patent must be granted before the plaintiff may bring action.[22] There are no rights which arise while a patent is pending. Note, however, that a patentee can claim reasonable compensation for use of an invention after the patent application is laid open to the public, but only if the patent actually issues.[23]

An action for infringement of a patent may be brought in either the Federal Court or in a provincial court of superior jurisdiction. An action to expunge or amend a patent must be brought in the Federal Court.

---

[16]   See s. 32 (PA).

[17]   See *Cutter (Canada) Ltd. v. Baxter Travenol Laboratories of Canada Ltd.* (1983), 72 C.P.R. (2d) 287 (S.C.C.); *Johnson Controls Inc. v. Varta Batteries Ltd.* (1984), 80 C.P.R. (2d) 1 (Fed. C.A.).

[18]   *Valmet Oy v. Beloit Canada Ltd.* (1988), 20 C.P.R. (3d) 1 (Fed. C.A.).

[19]   See s. 42 (PA).

[20]   See ss. 54, 55 and 57 (PA), which provide remedies by way of injunction, damages, accounts or delivery up and otherwise are available to the owner of the patent.

[21]   See *Leesona Corp. v. Reliable Hosiery Mills Ltd.* (1974), 14 C.P.R. (2d) 168 (Fed. T.D.).

[22]   For liability before publication, see s. 57 (PA). For liability after publication but before issue, see s. 55(2) (PA).

[23]   See s. 55(2) (PA).

4. Types of Things Protected

Patent protection is only available for inventions. An invention must be new and useful and may relate to

(a) a product;[24]

(b) a process;[25]

(c) an apparatus;[26] or

(d) a composition of matter.[27]

In addition, an invention must have inventive merit or be non-obvious to a person skilled in the art.

An invention may be a product, process,[28] composition of matter[29] or manufacture.[30]

Examples of things which are *not* inventions might include:

(a) a discovery (*e.g.*, discovery of a new element or substance);

(b) works of authorship;[31]

(c) mere scientific principles;[32]

(d) an abstract theorem;[33]

(e) a mathematical method;

(f) mere information, concepts or ideas;

(g) speculations, things not defined with precision or beyond reasonable prediction;[34]

---

[24]   A product is made of a novel combination of elements.

[25]   A process is a novel, logically interconnected series of steps to do something, such as, a method or way to make a chemical or algorithm, or a way to use a device.

[26]   An apparatus is a novel machine which can be used to make products or practise a process.

[27]   A composition of matter is a combination of elements which result in a novel substance.

[28]   For examples of processes, see *Tennessee Eastman Co. v. Canada (Commissioner of Patents)* (1972), [1974] S.C.R. 111, 8 C.P.R. (2d) 202 and *Burton Parsons Chemicals Inc. v. Hewlett-Packard (Can.) Ltd.* (1974), 17 C.P.R. (2d) 97 (S.C.C.).

[29]   For an example of a composition of matter, see *Shell Oil Co. v. Canada (Patents Commissioner)*, [1982] 2 S.C.R. 536, 67 C.P.R. (2d) 1.

[30]   For an example of a manufacture, see *Windsurfing International Inc. v. Trilantic Corp.* (1985), 8 C.P.R. (3d) 241 (Fed. C.A.).

[31]   See Chapter 2, "Copyright Law", for more details.

[32]   See s. 27(8) (PA).

[33]   See s. 27(8) (PA).

[34]   See *Re Application No. 178,117 for Patent by Farbwerke Hoechst AG* (1980), 13 C.P.R. (3d) 212 (Pat. App. Bd. & Pat. Commr.), revd (1985), 16 C.P.R. (3d) 91 (Fed. C.A.).

(h) computer programs *per se*;[35]

(i) aggregations, things where the elements do not work together;[36]

(j) a scheme or method of playing a game or doing business;[37]

(k) a method of accounting or providing statistics on IQ tests;

(l) things which do not work;

(m) things which serve no useful purpose or solve no practical problem;

(n) things which are not new or which are obvious;

(o) a mental act such as an approach to thinking;[38]

(p) an invention with an illicit or immoral purpose;

(q) colours (*i.e.*, in the absence of any other feature); or

(r) features or parts or components of an article which are solely visually appreciated.

An invention may be a new use for an old thing.[39]
Examples of some well-known inventions include:

(a) the Thermos brand vacuum bottle design;

(b) the machine to make Shredded Wheat brand cereal;

(c) the incandescent light bulb design;

(d) the original telephone design of Alexander Graham Bell; and

(e) the Windsurfer brand sail board design.

5. Formal Requirements for Protection

Patent protection is only available under a registry system. One must file and obtain the grant of a patent to have enforceable rights.[40]

---

[35] See 12.02.01(g) Manual of Patent Office Practice. Note, however, that an inventive process practised by a programmed computer may be patentable. See also s. 28(3) (PA) and *Schlumberger Canada Ltd. v. Canada (Patents Commissioner)* (1981), 56 C.P.R. (2d) 204 (Fed. C.A.), leave to appeal to S.C.C. refused (1981), 63 C.P.R. (2d) 261n.

[36] Examples of aggregations are: a pencil and eraser, a nut cracker and dish, and a cigarette lighter and ash tray.

[37] See 12.02.01(e) Manual of Patent Office Practice. See also *Cowan's Application*, 100 C.I.P.R. October 17, 1972 (Com'r Pat.).

[38] For an example of a process involving mental steps, see *Re Application of Itek Corp.* (1981), 68 C.P.R. (2d) 94 (Pat. App. Bd. & Pat. Commr.).

[39] See *Shell Oil Co. v. Canada (Patents Commissioner)*, *supra*, footnote 29.

[40] For details on the patent application process, see *Obtaining Patents*, Practice Guide (Toronto: Carswell, 1995).

Certain formal conditions must be satisfied in order to come within the protection of the *Patent Act*. Briefly these are:

(a) the invention must be protectable subject-matter;

(b) the invention must be new;

(c) the invention must be useful; and

(d) the invention must show sufficient inventive merit.

(a) Subject-Matter

To be patentable, the technology must not only be an invention but it must be appropriate subject-matter for patent protection. For reasons of public policy, certain inventions may not be patentable. For example:

(a) a method of medical treatment;[41]

(b) a computer program *per se*;[42] and

(c) certain living things.[43]

Inventors of pharmaceutical inventions in Canada are subject to stringent price review of the sale of the patented products by the Patented Medicine Prices Review Board.[44]

(b) Utility

Patent law is only intended to protect inventions which serve some useful purpose. Some technologies are speculative. The technology must solve some practical problem. The technology must work, it must do what the inventor claims it can do.[45] If it does not work it is not useful.[46]

---

[41] See *Tennessee Eastman Co. v. Canada (Commissioner of Patents)* (1972), [1974] S.C.R. 111, 8 C.P.R. (2d) 202: a surgical method of bonding tissues.

[42] See *Schlumberger Canada Ltd. v. Canada (Patents Commissioner)* (1981), 56 C.P.R. (2d) 204 (Fed. C.A.) leave to appeal to S.C.C. denied: a computer program. On the other hand, an inventive process practised by a programmed computer is patentable.

[43] Canada's patent office issues patents for unicellular organisms which are inventions. Canada lags behind its major trading partners in providing express protection of inventive higher life forms. In *Pioneer Hi-Bred Ltd. v. Canada (Commissioner of Patents)* (1987), 25 C.I.P.R. 1 (S.C.C.), a new soya bean variety created by selective cross-breeding was found not to be patentable because the disclosure requirements for patent protection were not met. The Court did not address the issue of patent protection of higher life forms. See Chapter 10, "Plant Breeders' Rights", for background on plant breeders' rights legislation available to protect plant varieties.

[44] See ss. 79-103 (PA) for details on the Patented Medicine Prices Review Board and its operations.

[45] *Consolboard Inc. v. MacMillan Bloedel (Sask.) Ltd.*, [1981] 1 S.C.R. 504, 56 C.P.R. (2d) 146.

[46] See, for example, *Prentice v. Dominion Rubber Co.*, [1928] Ex. C.R. 196 (Ex. Ct.).

In addition, there should be no breach of a fundamental law of science.[47] For example, a perpetual motion machine violates the second law of thermodynamics. In such cases it is unlikely that the proposed technology actually works.

(c) Novelty

An invention must satisfy a requirement of novelty in order to be capable of being granted patent protection. An invention must be the first in the world. It must be new. To be protectable the invention must be new[48] and

(a) not anticipated by another event or document which shows the same thing;

(b) not anticipated by another event or document which describes essentially the same thing for practical purposes; and

(c) not available to the public.[49]

For example, the application of a known method to known materials but where the method had never before been previously applied to such materials may be novel.[50] For purposes of attacking novelty, the prior art should

(a) give an exact prior description;

(b) give directions which will inevitably result in something in the claims;

(c) give clear and unmistakable directions to make the thing;

---

[47]   See, for example, *Minerals Separation North American Corp. v. Noranda Mines Ltd.* (1952), 15 C.P.R. 133 (Can. P.C.).

[48]   Any discussions by which the elements of the invention become available to the public may subject to the use of the grace period (discussed below), adversely affect prospects for patent protection. Disclosures under a secrecy agreement in Canada have been seen as not damaging patentability. See *Procter & Gamble Co. v. Bristol-Myers Canada Ltd.* (1978), 39 C.P.R. (2d) 145 (Fed. T.D.), affd (1979), 42 C.P.R. (2d) 33, 28 N.R. 273 (Fed. C.A.), leave to appeal to S.C.C. refused (1979), 42 C.P.R. (2d) 33n (S.C.C.).

[49]   Comparing an invention with a prior invention involves:

　　(a) examining each of the elements of the invention;

　　(b) looking at the invention as a whole;

　　(c) identifying the relevant prior art;

　　(d) reviewing the prior art in the context of what would be understood by a person skilled in the art (see below for the level of skill expected of such a person); and

　　(e) for the purposes of assessing novelty, one may not make a mosaic of the documents (*i.e.*, one must find the same thing or the same thing for practical purposes in one document).

For an example see *Windsurfing International Inc. v. Trilantic Corp.* (1985), 8 C.P.R. (3d) 241 (Fed. C.A.), additional reasons at (1986), 8 C.P.R. (3d) 270 (Fed. C.A.).

[50]   See *Canada (Commissioner of Patents) v. Ciba Ltd.*, [1959] S.C.R. 378.

(d) give information which for purposes of practical utility is equal to that given by the subject patent;

(e) give information so a person struggling with the same problem finds an answer;

(f) give information to a person of ordinary knowledge so the person at once perceives the invention; or

(g) teach an inevitable result which can only be proved by experiment.[51]

To be protectable an application for a patent in the Canadian Patent Office must have been filed:

(a) For foreign patent applications filed under convention or treaty rights:

(i) before any application for a patent describing the same invention was filed in Canada by any other person before the priority or claim date of the foreign application, or

(ii) before an application for a patent describing the same invention and which is filed as a convention or treaty application in Canada by any other person at any time and the priority or claim date of that convention or treaty application precedes the priority date of the foreign application.[52]

(b) For all other patent applications filed:

(i) the application must be filed before any application for a patent describing the same invention was filed in Canada by any other person,[53] or

(ii) the application must be filed before any application for a patent describing the same invention and which is a convention or treaty application is filed in Canada by any other person and the priority date of which convention application precedes the priority date of the application.[54]

(c) Except for the limited disclosures by the inventor or through the inventor, the invention must not have been disclosed by any person such that the

---

[51] See, for example, *Johnson Controls Inc. v. Varta Batteries Ltd.* (1984), 80 C.P.R. (2d) 1 (Fed. C.A.): a battery case invention, and citing from *Reeves Brothers Inc. v. Toronto Quilting & Embroidery Ltd.* (1978), 43 C.P.R. (2d) 145 (Fed. T.D.), and cases cited therein. The recited list is language drawn from older cases seeking to address issues of novelty. With respect, the comments suggesting all of these listed items must be satisfied, are incorrect.

[52] See s. 28(1) (PA) defining the claim date. See s. 28.2(1)(*d*)(i)(B) (PA).

[53] See s. 28.2(1)(*c*) (PA).

[54] See ss. 28.2(1)(*d*)(i) and 28.2(1)(*d*)(ii) (PA).

invention became available to the public before the date of filing of the application or the priority date of the application.[55]

(d) The inventor or a person who obtained knowledge of the invention from the inventor may disclose the invention such that it becomes available to the public in Canada or elsewhere but only if such disclosure occurred *no more than one year before the filing of the application*.[56]

The novelty rules in the United States are different. Generally to be able to make a valid patent application in the United States Patent and Trade-mark Office, the application must:

(a) not have been made available to the public in the United States more than one year before the application is filed in the United States Patent and Trade-mark Office, and

(b) not have been described in a printed publication anywhere more than one year before the application is filed in the United States Patent and Trade-mark Office.[57]

In many countries no disclosure which results in the invention being made available to the public in that country or elsewhere (including in Canada) may be carried out before a valid patent application is filed in that country's patent office. Typically an inventor may seek to use convention priority to manage the filing of the patent application in foreign countries including managing foreign filings in relation to public disclosure of the invention subsequent to the first (priority) application (See Chapter 14, "International Treaties", for a detailed introduction to the use of convention priority).

(d) Inventive Merit

The requirement to show some inventive merit in a technology has been judicially developed.[58] To be an invention a technology must not be obvious to a person skilled in the art. The applicable art is that related to the invention. For example, if the invention is a device in the oil and gas industry then the applicable art should be that industry or any directly-related industry.[59]

---

[55] See s. 28.2(1)(*b*) (PA).

[56] See s. 28.2(1)(*a*) (PA). Note that use of the "grace period" contemplated in that paragraph may result in loss of ability to obtain patent protection in many foreign countries.

[57] Note that use of the "grace period" contemplated under the American patent law may result in loss of ability to obtain patent protection in many foreign countries.

[58] See *Beloit Canada Ltée/Ltd. v. Valmet Oy* (1986), 8 C.P.R. (3d) 289 (Fed. C.A.), leave to appeal to S.C.C. refused (1986), 8 C.I.P.R. xlvii (note) (S.C.C.).

[59] For examples of what the non-obviousness should relate to, see *Xerox of Canada Ltd. v. IBM Canada Ltd.* (1977), 33 C.P.R. (2d) 24 (Fed. T.D.). For an example of the extent of

In Canada the notional person skilled in the art is an unimaginative skilled technician.[60] The test for obviousness can be stated as follows: in light of the prior art of which the person skilled in the art would be aware at the time the invention was made and with the skilled person's general knowledge in addition to information and literature available to the person at the time, would the unimaginative skilled technician have come directly and without difficulty to the invention?[61]

This is a difficult test to apply. One must ascertain the following:

(a) What is the relevant art?

(b) Who is the notional unimaginative skilled technician?

(c) What is the level of knowledge of the notional unimaginative skilled technician?

(d) What information and general knowledge would be available to such a person in the relevant art?

One should not rely on hindsight analysis.[62] Since inventions often appear obvious once revealed, one often looks to certain objective indications which suggest the invention was not obvious before the application was filed. The test applied by the court is an objective test.[63]

Some such indications of non-obviousness are:

(a) other persons did not assess likelihood of success of the unmade invention so as to warrant a test or trial of the technology;

(b) prior work in the field points to a different solution;

(c) the industry (art) thought it would not work;

---

non-obviousness required, see *Reading & Bates Construction Co. v. Baker Energy Resources Corp.* (1987), 17 C.I.P.R. 199, 18 C.P.R. (3d) 180 (Fed. C.A.).

[60] For discussion of the art, see *Shell Oil Co. v. Canada (Patent Commissioner)*, [1982] 2 S.C.R. 536, 67 C.P.R. (2d) 1. In the United States the notional person skilled in the art is an ordinary skilled person.

[61] For examples, see *Procter & Gamble Co. v. Calgon Interamerican Corp.* (1982), 61 C.P.R. (2d) 1 (Fed. C.A.); *Baxter Travenol Laboratories of Canada Ltd. v. Cutter Ltd.* (1983), 68 C.P.R. (2d) 179 (Fed. C.A.): a blood bag collections system; *Windsurfing International Inc. v. Trilantic Corp.* (1985), 8 C.P.R. (3d) 241 (Fed. C.A.): a sailing board; *Reading & Bates Construction Co. v. Baker Energy Resources Corp., supra*, footnote 59: a liner invention and a pull-back invention used in a pre-bored path with a view to installing a pipeline.

[62] See *Reading & Bates Construction Co. v. Baker Energy Resources Corp., supra*, footnote 59. There, the following example of the expression that one is "wiser after the fact" is noted: "Nothing is easier to say, after the event, that the thing was obvious and involved no invention": *Non-Drip Measure Co. v. Stranger's Ltd.* (1943), 60 R.P.C. 135 (H.L.).

[63] *Reading & Bates Construction Co. v. Baker Energy Resources Corp., supra*, footnote 59.

(d) the invention meets an unfulfilled need in the marketplace;[64]

(e) substantial commercial success of the invention;[65] or

(f) substantial infringement of the invention.[66]

6. Term of Protection

A patent based on an application filed on or after October 1, 1989 is granted for twenty years from the date of application.[67] A patent based on an application filed before October 1, 1989 is granted for seventeen years from the date of issue of the patent.[68] The term of patents based on applications filed on or after October 1, 1989 may be limited if maintenance fees are not paid within the time provided.[69]

Once the term expires, the rights of the patentee end and the invention may be used, manufactured and sold by any person. The expiry of a base patent does not, however, affect the rights which may exist in improvement which have been patented subsequently.

7. Ownership of the Rights

The basic principle is that the inventor is the owner of the invention.[70] Only the inventor or his or her legal representative may apply for a patent in respect of the invention.[71]

---

[64] The argument is that if the need existed a reasonable period of time before the application was filed and if the invention was obvious, then someone would have made the invention before. Since no one made the invention before, it must have been non-obvious.

[65] The argument is that substantial commercial success is an indication that there was an unfulfilled need in the marketplace which has been addressed by the invention, as noted above.

[66] The argument is that substantial infringement is an indication that there was an unfulfilled need in the marketplace which has been addressed by the invention and which the inventor has not been able to fulfil him or herself resulting in the infringing activity by the defendants.

[67] See s. 44 (PA).

[68] See s. 45 (PA).

[69] See s. 46(2) (PA).

[70] Note that the *Patent Act* is silent on the ownership of an invention. The law regarding ownership of inventions has been developed by the courts.

[71] See s. 27(1) (PA).

The identity of the inventor[72] is a question of fact and is tested against the claims in the patent.[73] Merely advancing an idea or suggestion in terms of an objective or an end result is not, by itself, inventorship.[74] The date of invention is that date when the inventor can prove he or she first formulated either in writing or orally a description which affords the means of making that which is invented.[75] The invention must originate in the inventor's mind, not be borrowed from elsewhere.[76]

(a) Hired to Invent

The general rule is that if a servant, while in the employ of his or her master, makes an invention, that invention belongs to the servant and not the master.[77] There are two lines of cases dealing with situations where an employee is hired to make inventions. The older cases hold that it is an implied term in a contract of employment that an employee is a trustee for his or her employer of any invention made in the course of employment unless there is an agreement to the contrary.[78] Some newer cases look more specifically at the scope of the employment and if the employee's work is not to make inventions or advance technology then the employee owns the invention.[79]

A current expression of the principles applicable are that an employee will own an invention unless:

(a) there is an agreement to the contrary,

(b) where the person was employed for the express purpose of inventing or innovating, or

(c) where the person is under a fiduciary or similar obligation to the employer.

---

[72] A misnomer of the inventor does not *per se* affect the validity of a patent especially where the patentee holds all rights of all inventors. See *Dec International Inc. v. A.L. LaCombe & Associates Ltd.* (1989), 26 C.P.R. (3d) 193 (Fed. T.D.); *Procter & Gamble Co. v. Bristol-Myers Canada Ltd.* (1978), 39 C.P.R. (2d) 145 (Fed. T.D.), affd (1979), 42 C.P.R. (2d) 33 (Fed. C.A.), leave to appeal to S.C.C. refused (1979), 42 C.P.R. (2d) 33n (S.C.C.).

[73] See *Ernest Scragg & Sons Ltd. v. Leesona Corp.* (1964), 45 C.P.R. 1 (Ex. Ct.).

[74] See, for example, *Comstock Canada v. Electec Ltd.* (1991), 38 C.P.R. (3d) 29 (Fed. T.D.).

[75] See, for example, *Rice v. Christiani & Nielsen*, [1930] 4 D.L.R. 401 (S.C.C.), affd [1931] A.C. 770 (P.C.); *Comstock Canada v. Electec Ltd.*, *supra*, footnote 74.

[76] See, for example, *Gerrard Wire Tying Machines Co. v. Cary Manufacturing Co.*, [1926] 3 D.L.R. 374 (Ex. Ct.); *Comstock Canada v. Electec Ltd.*, *supra*, footnote 74.

[77] See, for example, *Bloxam v. Elsee* (1827), 108 E.R. 415 (H.L.); *W.J. Gage Ltd. v. Sugden*, [1967] 2 O.R. 151 (H.C.); *Comstock Canada v. Electec Ltd.*, *supra*, footnote 74.

[78] See *Patchett v. Sterling Engineering Co.* (1955), 72 R.P.C. 50 (H.L.), approved and adopted in *W.J. Gage Ltd. v. Sugden, supra*, footnote 77.

[79] See *Comstock Canada v. Electec Ltd.*, *supra*, footnote 74.

Factors considered by the court may include:

(a) whether the employee was hired for the express purpose of inventing;

(b) whether the employee at the time he or she was hired had previously made inventions;

(c) whether an employer had incentive plans encouraging product development;

(d) whether the conduct of the employee once the invention has been created suggested ownership by the employer;

(e) whether the invention is the product of the problem the employee was instructed to solve, *i.e.*, was it his or her duty to make inventions?

(f) whether the employee's invention arose following his or her consultation through normal company channels (*i.e.*, was help sought?);

(g) whether the employee was dealing with highly confidential information or confidential work; and

(h) whether it was a term of the employee's employment that he or she could not use the ideas which he or she developed to his or her own advantage.[80]

The *Patent Act* provides special rules for inventions made by officers, servants or employees of the Crown or of a corporation that is an agent or servant of the Crown.[81] In such cases if the person makes the invention within the scope of his or her duties and employment, related to munitions of war, all benefits of the invention and any patent which issued in relation to the invention are assigned to the Minister of National Defence.[82]

(b) Fiduciaries

An inventor may be obligated to assign his or her invention to a person (typically an employer) with whom the inventor has a fiduciary or similar relationship.[83] Care must be exercised to determine if the inventor is in such a relationship of high trust. The mere fact that an inventor held a senior position in a company does not deprive the inventor of an invention if that is not what the inventor was hired to do.[84] A manager's position is radically different from that of a tradesman. The manager has a fundamental or fiduciary duty to

---

[80]   *Supra.*

[81]   Inventions made by Crown employees may be governed by the *Public Servants Inventions Act*, R.S.C. 1985, c. P-32. See also s. 20 (PA) regarding government-owned inventions.

[82]   See s. 20 (PA).

[83]   See, for example, *Comstock Canada v. Electec Ltd., supra,* footnote 74.

[84]   *Anemostat (Scotland) Ltd. v. Michaelis*, [1957] R.P.C. 167.

extend effort, skill, knowledge and inventive powers, in whatever way possible, to promote the efficiency and success of the employer and does not need to be specifically directed or encouraged to do so.[85] Similarly, a director or senior officer is precluded from obtaining for him or herself, either secretly or without the approval of the company, any property or business advantage belonging to the company or for which it has been negotiating.[86]

(c) Shop Right

Some American cases have developed the concept of a "shop right". This is a non-exclusive right of an employer to use an invention made by and owned by an employee where the invention was made with the employer's tools or resources. This concept has not been well-received in Canadian law.[87] There are several cases which have appeared to find implied rights of an employer to use an employee's invention.[88]

(d) Contract to the Contrary

If the parties enter into a written agreement specifically and expressly addressing the ownership of the rights in the invention, the courts will give force to that agreement.

8. Special Rules

(a) Co-existence with Other Rights

Note that trade-mark protection for the brand name of the product made using or related to the invention has been used to capture the goodwill related to the invention. Trade-mark rights can continue past the expiry of the patent rights.[89]

It has been suggested that copyright does not extend to drawings in patent specifications.[90] Patent protection does not co-exist with trade secret law.

---

[85]   See *Worthington Pumping Engine Co. v. Moore* (1902), 20 R.P.C. 41 (U.K. Ch.); *Edisonia Ltd. v. Forse* (1908), 25 R.P.C. 546 (U.K. Ch.); *Canadian Aero Service Ltd. v. O'Malley* (1973), 11 C.P.R. (2d) 206 (S.C.C.), cited as authority for this proposition in *Comstock Canada v. Electec Ltd., supra,* footnote 74.

[86]   *Canadian Aero Service Ltd. v. O'Malley, supra,* footnote 85.

[87]   See *W.J. Gage Ltd. v. Sugden, supra,* footnote 77.

[88]   See *Imperial Supply Co. v. Grand Trunk Railway* (1912), 14 Ex. C.R. 88 (Ex. Ct.); *Willard's Chocolates Ltd. v. Bardsley* (1928), 35 O.W.N. 92 (H.C.).

[89]   See Chapter 7, "Trade-marks".

[90]   See *Rucker Co. v. Gavel's Vulcanizing Ltd.* (1985), 6 C.I.P.R. 137 (Fed. T.D.), vard (1987), 14 C.P.R. (3d) 439 (Fed. T.D.).

(b) Notice

The placement of a specific patent notice is not required under Canadian law. The placement of a notice is prudent as it provides a warning of the claim to certain rights and identifies the owner. It might be argued that placing an accurate notice provides notice of the patentee's rights which may facilitate the patent owner's ability to claim punitive damages in an appropriate case. The statement "patent pending" or "patent applied for" may be applied to articles after the patent application has been filed. These notices have no legal effect except as a warning of the possible existence of rights.

It may be an offence under the patent laws of several countries (such as the United States and United Kingdom) to place a notice falsely claiming to have filed a patent application. While no such prohibition exists for Canada, caution is suggested due to the provisions of s. 75 of the *Patent Act* which provides for certain offences where one:

(a) without the consent of the patentee, places the patentee's name or an imitation thereof on anything made by the person, or

(b) without the consent of the patentee marks "patented", "Letters Patent", "Queen's (or King's) Patent", "Patented" on anything with an intent to imitate any mark of the patentee or of deceiving the public that the thing was produced with the consent of the patentee.

(c) International Filings

By virtue of the Convention for the Protection of Industrial Property made in Paris (Paris Convention), an applicant for patent protection may file a corresponding application in the appropriate government office of other member countries and claim the priority of the first filing date but only if such subsequent filings are made within one year of the first filing date.

Canada also adheres to the Patent Co-operation Treaty which provides a similar method of managing foreign filings.

Some details on the Paris Convention and the Patent Co-operation Treaty and operation and use of convention priority may be found in Chapter 14, "International Treaties". Canadian applicants making their first filing for an invention must therefore be aware that foreign applications filed up to one year before the Canadian application is filed may have priority to obtain the grant of a patent for the invention.

13

Utility Models

1. What are Utility Models?

Related to industrial design and patent law, the rights which may be obtained in a utility model provide protection for useful designs which do not meet the high test of patent protection. Some countries call this form of protection petty patents or utility models.

Canada has no system for the protection of utility models. As a result, for mass-produced articles:

(a) if a designer's work appeals to the eye, the designer may seek industrial design protection; and

(b) if a designer's work is useful, the designer may seek either trade secret or patent protection but if the high standard of patentability cannot be met and secrecy cannot be maintained, there appears to be little protection available for the designer.

There are few alternatives. Limited protection may be available for trademarks used in the useful designs but not protection for the investment and creative efforts involved in making the design itself. Intellectual property rights are not available for all types of creative expression regardless of the effort, cost and investment involved in the creative process. Economic and historical factors dominate the form and extent of protection available for specific forms of creativity.

Historically, creativity expressed in subjects of engineering or the sciences (such as useful designs or inventions) is generally only protected for substantial and significant advances over prior advances[1] and little or no protection is available for creativity which does not meet the high standard required for patent protection.

---

[1] See, for example, s. 64(3) (CA) and s. 5(1) (IDA) which limit protection available for utilitarian functions of designs.

Fundamentally, and in most cases, creativity expressed in useful things which do not meet the high level of creativity required under patent law or is not protectable under trade secret law is unprotected in Canada.

14

International Treaties

1. Introduction

Intellectual property rights can provide substantial barriers to trade. Since such rights can create monopolies they can be used to limit international trade if common standards are not applied by the trading nations. As a result, a number of major multilateral treaties provide for a minimum set of standards applicable to certain forms of intellectual property. While many international treaties exist, the most important are the requirements of the GATT Trade Related Aspects of International Property Rights ("TRIPS") agreements, the Universal Copyright Convention, the Berne Convention, the Paris Convention and the Patent Co-operation Treaty. These treaties are discussed below.

The major conventions operate on a national treatment basis. That means that a Canadian's work will be treated no differently than that of a national of another member country. So, for example, a copyrighted work is protected in Germany under German copyright law, in Japan under Japanese copyright law and Canada under Canadian copyright law.

2. GATT TRIPS

The importance of intellectual property in trade relations was confirmed with the adoption of minimum mandatory standards of selected forms of intellectual property rights. In particular the adoption of the TRIPS agreement as part of the Uruguay Round of the Multilateral Trade Negotiations[1] mandates all members of the World Trade Organization to adhere to the minimum standards established by the Berne Convention (for copyright) and the Paris Convention (for designs, trademarks and patents). Both the Paris Convention and Berne Convention are described below.

---

[1] See Final Act Embodying the Results of the Uruguay Round of Multilateral Trade Negotiations, done at Marrakech, Morocco, April 15, 1994, Annex 1C: Agreement on Trade-Related Aspects of Intellectual Property Rights, April 15, 1994.

In addition, the TRIPS agreement provides an important guarantee of enforcement procedures to be available under the national laws of member countries.[2] Historically, some countries might provide availability of rights but no effective means to enforce those rights. The new minimum enforcement procedures may be the most substantial achievement of this agreement as it mandates some level of meaningful enforcement of certain intellectual property rights for international rights holders.

Other important advances of the TRIPS agreement include the establishment of uniform minimum standards of protection in the field of patent law. Member countries can no longer discriminate against specific forms of technology for patent protection and may not discriminate in respect of where an invention was made.[3] Each member country will provide a twenty-year term of patent protection (from the date of application or priority). In addition, the patent owner is to have the right to supply a market for the patented product with imported products.[4]

The TRIPS agreement extends the Paris Convention trademark provisions to services.[5] Protection was also provided for geographic indications of source[6] and specific anticounterfeiting measures.[7] In the copyright field rental rights for sound recordings and some more standardized protection for computer programs is required. Some efforts were made in seeking to move towards the protection of neighbouring rights as provided in the Rome Convention such as minimum standards of protection for broadcasters, performers and phonogram producers.[8]

The TRIPS agreement provided the first international protection for confidential information.[9]

---

[2]   See, *ibid.*, arts. 41-50.

[3]   See, *ibid.*, art. 27(1). Note that this seeks to end the United States' historical discrimination against foreigners in establishing an invention date for the purpose of priority of the application.

[4]   See, *ibid.*, art. 28(1). Note that this new right appears to conflict with Article 5 A of the Paris Convention which requires the local working of a patent.

[5]   See, *ibid.*, art. 16(2).

[6]   See, *ibid.*, art. 22(1).

[7]   See, *ibid.*, arts. 41-50.

[8]   See *An Act to Amend the Copyright Act*, S.C. 1997, c. 24, which seeks to implement many of these changes.

[9]   See, *op. cit.*, footnote 2, s. 7 and art. 39(1).

3. Universal Copyright Convention

Until recently, a significant reason for inclusion of a copyright notice on a work was to take advantage of the Universal Copyright Convention[10] ("UCC") and seek to establish a claim for copyright protection in the United States. The UCC requires the following form of copyright notice to be prominently displayed on a work:

©   year of publication   name of owner.

An example of the notice is:

©   1998   Martin Kratz.

The © symbol is specifically mandated by the UCC. The year is the year of first publication of the work. The name is the identity of the copyright owner. This form of copyright notice is also recognized as a proper notice under the domestic copyright law of the United States.

Given the importance of the American market for many Canadian works, it may be important to seek to avoid inadvertent loss of rights in the United States as a result of the operation of the American domestic rules. The case of the United States is important because of its close proximity to Canada and also because of the way American law may treat certain foreign works. Under the Berne Convention (see Section 4, "Berne Convention", *infra*) the United States is required to provide automatic copyright protection without formalities to works of nationals of Berne Convention members. The American copyright law does this by distinguishing between domestic works (which must comply with the more complex American domestic rules) and Berne Convention works which receive automatic protection without formalities. A Canadian work may be considered an American domestic work if it is either first published or "simultaneously published" in the United States. A work is considered to be simultaneously published in the United States if it is published in the United States within ninety days of being first published elsewhere.

Placement of a UCC notice prominently on a work provides a basis for a copyright claim in the UCC member countries which are not members of the Berne Convention.[11]

---

[10]   Adopted at Geneva (1951), revised at Paris (1971). Canada joined this treaty on August 10, 1962. For a list of members of this treaty see the appendices to *Protection of Copyright and Industrial Design*, Practice Guide, (Toronto: Carswell, 1995), where it is possible to verify the continued status of any applicable country under the treaty.

[11]   Russia, Ukraine, Kazakstan and Belarus for example.

4. Berne Convention

Canada is signatory to the Convention for the protection of literary and artistic works made in Berne.[12] This is the most important international copyright treaty. The Berne Convention provides for automatic copyright protection to nationals of each member country without any requirement of formalities.

A significant recent member of the Berne Convention is the United States of America, which joined in late 1988, effective March 1, 1989. As a result, for works published or produced after March 1, 1989, Canadian copyright claimants are able to claim the benefit of the Berne Convention in order to claim copyright protection in the United States (see Section 3, "Universal Copyright Convention", *supra*).

In the absence of proof to the contrary, the placement of the author's name on a work provides for a useful presumption that the author is the copyright holder.[13] The placement of the UCC notice on a work does not impair the ability to claim rights under the Berne Convention.

5. Paris Convention

Canada is a member of the Paris Convention for the protection of industrial property.[14] Nationals of member countries may utilize the provisions of the convention to facilitate their foreign filings in other member countries of the convention.

This convention operates to permit an applicant to file an application for registration of certain rights in one country and file corresponding applications in other member countries of the convention, so long as the corresponding applications are filed within a specific period of the first application. By relying on the convention the applicant has a priority date (the

---

[12]   Berne Convention (1886); completed at Paris (1896); revised at Berlin (1908); completed at Berne (1914); revised at Rome (1928); at Brussels (1948); at Stockholm (1967); and at Paris (1971); and amended in 1979 (Berne Union). Canada joined this convention on April 10, 1928 and adheres to the Rome text as of August 1, 1931 and the Stockholm text, arts. 22-38, as of July 7, 1970.

For a list of members of this treaty see the appendices to *Protection of Copyright and Industrial Design, op. cit.*, footnote 10, where it is possible to verify the continued status of any applicable country under the treaty.

[13]   See art. 15, Berne Convention.

[14]   Paris Convention of March 20, 1883, made effective July 7, 1884; Revised at Brussels, December 14, 1900; revised at Washington, June 2, 1911; revised at the Hague, November 6, 1925; revised at London, June 2, 1934; revised at Lisbon, October 31, 1958; revised at Stockholm, July 14, 1967; amended in 1979. Canada joined this treaty on September 1, 1923 and adheres to the Stockholm text. For a list of members of this treaty see the appendices to *Obtaining Patents*, Practice Guide (Toronto: Carswell, 1995), where it is possible to verify the continued status of any applicable country under the treaty.

date of the first filing) and can claim that priority date in other member countries so long as the corresponding applications are filed within the applicable period.

In effect this allows an applicant to back-date an application filed in other countries *as if* they were filed on the priority date and thereby have an application with a priority date *before* any public disclosure activity.[15]

In the case of industrial designs or trademarks, the applicable period is six months. In the case of patents, the applicable period is one year.

An example involving efforts to seek patent protection may illustrate how the convention might operate. If an applicant wishes to protect his or her invention in several countries, considerable upfront costs may be incurred. By use of the convention, an applicant can file first in one country, say, Canada, and defer the filing in the other convention member countries (within the twelve months) and still claim the date of the first filing (in Canada) in those other countries. This arrangement permits an applicant to defer the costs of the subsequent filings for some time.

_x_____y_____Time

First Filing   Subsequent Filings

& Costs   & Related Costs

To claim priority filings, y must occur less than twelve months after filing x.

The convention permits the applicant to claim the earliest filing date as the priority date and therefore seek to have the same priority in each country. The convention may not work to preserve an ability to obtain patent protection if there was prior public disclosure or the invention became available to the public before the first (priority) application is filed.

6. Patent Co-operation Treaty

Canada is a member of the Patent Co-operation Treaty ("PCT").[16] The PCT applies only to patent applications and like the Paris Convention, assists an applicant to manage foreign filings. The application of the PCT rules have received little judicial consideration in Canada as they are relatively new here. The PCT consists of two phases, an international phase and a national phase.

---

[15]   If there was public disclosure activity before the first filing, one must review the domestic law of each country in order to determine whether or not a valid application may still be filed. The use of convention priority works best if the first (priority) application is filed before any public activity with an invention or design anywhere. In all other cases one would review the availability, if any, of rights due to the prior public activity under the domestic law of the countries involved.

[16]   PCT made in Washington 1970; amended in 1979 and modified in 1984. Canada joined the PCT on January 2, 1990. For a list of members of this treaty, see the appendices to *Obtaining Patents, op. cit.*, footnote 14, and verify the continued status of any applicable country under the treaty.

The PCT is administered by the World Intellectual Property Organization ("WIPO").

Like the Paris Convention, PCT permits the applicant to delay filing corresponding applications in other member countries. Under PCT the patent applicant can delay the filing of corresponding patent applications up to twenty or even thirty months.

Another similarity to the Paris Convention is that PCT does not eliminate the need to comply with the requirements of domestic law in each country or prosecute the application in each country. Unlike the Paris Convention, PCT may facilitate the decision-making of the applicant during prosecution and may facilitate to a degree such prosecutions of the application. The PCT and Paris Convention may work together. Filing under PCT does not preclude the applicant from claiming rights under the Paris Convention.

(a) The International Phase

The international phase begins with the filing of a single patent application in a PCT member country's "Receiving Office". Filing permits the applicant to designate other PCT member countries to which the filing shall relate. Note that designating more than ten countries does not require a designation fee. Note, however, that designation may result in costs arising in that country as the PCT application moves to the national phase.

This international application may be in English or other official language of PCT. The international fees are paid once and there is no need at this stage to be concerned about the formal requirements of each designated country's patent office. Unlike the Paris Convention, there is no need to provide each country's patent office with original drawings or certified copies of the priority application.

An international search is carried out by one of the "international searching authorities". The search is carried out using patent records of several major patent offices. An international search report is prepared based on the results of the search. The international search report and the application (and any amendments made thereto) are published by the international bureau of WIPO eighteen months after the priority date. The international search report and the application (and any amendments made thereto) are transmitted to each of the national patent offices designated by the applicant by the international bureau of WIPO. This would begin the national phase of PCT.

An applicant using PCT can file first in one country, say, Canada, and defer the specific filing costs in the other PCT member countries which have been designated for up to twenty months and still claim the date of the first filing (in Canada) in those other countries. This arrangement permits an applicant to defer the costs of the translations, filing fees and related expenses required in each designated country for some time.

If the applicant wishes, he or she can request an international preliminary examination. This has the effect of delaying the entry into the national phase an additional ten months, for a total deferral of thirty months.

(b) Preliminary Examination Report

The applicant under the PCT has the option to request an international preliminary examination. Countries designated in the PCT application and in which the applicant has requested a preliminary examination report are said to be "elected states". The request for an international preliminary examination must be made within nineteen months of the priority filing date. The international preliminary examination is carried out by an "international preliminary examining authority" designated under PCT.

The international preliminary examination report is provided to the applicant. It is a confidential document and will not be provided to a third party without the applicant's express authorization. Like the international search report, the international preliminary examination report, if provided to the examiner, is not binding on the national patent offices.

International preliminary examinations serve to formulate a preliminary and non-binding opinion on whether or not the invention appears to be novel, to satisfy requirements of utility and whether there appears to be an inventive step (*i.e.*, it is non-obvious). The report is typically received twenty-eight months after the filing date of the application. This gives the applicant two months to review the opinion in the report before the application proceeds to the national phase.

The major effects of requesting an international preliminary examination are:

(a) the entry of the application into the national phase is delayed up to a further ten months (for a maximum total deferral of thirty months); and

(b) the applicant receives a report which addresses the substance of the application and may aid the applicant in determining whether or not to proceed, whether to seek to amend the application and the like. This information is acquired before the onset of the national phase and the applicant's requirement to incur substantial national filing fees and translation costs.

(c) The National Phase

At the conclusion of the international phase the applicant must decide whether or not to process with filings in each country he or she has designated. This is called the national phase of the PCT. When the application enters the national phase, the applicant must:

(a) pay national (or regional) filing fees;

(b) provide any translations of the application if required by the national patent office; and

(c) appoint a local agent, where required, to prosecute the national application.

Depending on the commercial prospects for the invention and the results of the international search report and, as applicable, the international preliminary examination report, the applicant may choose not to proceed in some designated countries and therefore not incur the national costs associated with that country.

The patent application must be prosecuted before each designated country. Each national patent office will apply its own rules and procedure to the application.

(d) Summary

A simplified example of how PCT works including a request for the optional international preliminary examination is shown below:

	x	z	a	b	c	d	y
				International Phase			National Phase
months	0	12		18	19	28	30
action taken	First filing and costs	Search	Report	Publication		Report and related costs	Commence National Phase

The PCT permits the applicant to claim the priority of filing x for up to thirty months after filing x.[17] The applicant designates those PCT member countries in which he or she wishes to secure patent protection on filing x. The applicant must review patent protection in non-PCT and non-Paris Convention countries or other situations where an immediate filing is desired at the time the priority application (x) is filed. The applicant may wish to file corresponding patent applications in non-PCT countries or non-designated PCT countries which are members of the Paris Convention. This must be done before the expiry of twelve months (z) after the priority application (x) was filed. The international search report (a) is published (b) eighteen months after the application is filed. The request for an international preliminary examination (c) (optional) must be filed before the nineteenth month after filing x. The report arising from the international preliminary examination (d) (optional) is provided to the applicant typically nine months after the request

---

17   Note that the above example presumes no disentitling public activity occurred prior to the priority filing date (x). If such disclosures occurred, then the use of the Paris Convention and PCT are severely and adversely affected.

and therefore before the entry into the national phase. Note the publication of the application and search report at eighteen months and its impact on subsequent filings.

15

Contracts In Restraint Of Trade

1. Introduction

The subject of the enforceability of contracts made in restraint of trade are not strictly related to intellectual property law. The subject is often covered in an intellectual property course since these types of restrictions, like intellectual property rights, serve to control and shape competition.

Historically and generally, a contract in restraint of trade is void as against the public policy in favour of competition and the ability of an individual to earn a livelihood.[1] Over time, limited exceptions evolved to this rule. We examine these exceptions in this chapter.

2. Enforceable Restraints

Unless a contract restraining trade can be upheld under the exceptions, (see, *infra*) such a restriction is void as being contrary to public policy.

In order to be enforceable, a contract restricting a person from engaging in any business must be reasonable both from the perspective of the parties and the interest protected and from the public interest. In addition, the restriction must be reasonable in the scope of restriction, the geographic area in which the restraint applies and in the duration of the restriction.

---

[1] See, for further background, *Saltman Engineering Co. v. Campbell Engineering Co.*, [1963] 3 All E.R. 413, 65 R.P.C. 203 (U.K. C.A.) and *Seager v. Copydex Ltd.*, [1967] 1 W.L.R. 923, [1967] R.P.C. 349, [1967] 2 All E.R. 415 (U.K. C.A.), and cases cited therein.

(a) Scope of Restriction

The restriction must be reasonable having regard to the interest being protected and must relate to that interest.[2] Most covenants in restraint of trade are found to be enforceable in order to protect against disclosure or misuse of confidential information[3] or from competition in respect of the sale of a business.[4] Such restrictions relate to competitive behaviour or misuse of the trade secrets, as applicable. Efforts to restrict activity in which the party has no legitimate interest to protect (*i.e.*, sale of non-competing products) will not be enforceable.

(b) Geography of the Restriction

The restriction must be reasonable having regard to the geographic area in which the restriction applies and in relation to interest being protected.[5] Efforts to restrict activity in a geographic area in which the party has no legitimate interest to protect (*i.e.*, sale of competing products in a marketplace where the restricting party is not engaged in business) will not be enforceable.

(c) Duration of Restraint

The restriction must be reasonable in relation to the duration of the period restrained and the interest being protected.[6] Efforts to restrict activity for longer than a reasonable period will not be enforceable.[7]

---

[2]   See, for example, *Saskatchewan Co-operative Wheat Producers Ltd. v. Zurowski*, [1926] 3 D.L.R. 810 (Sask. C.A.); *Esso Petroleum Co. v. Harper's Garage (Stourport) Ltd.*, [1967] 1 All E.R. 699 (H.L.); *Garbutt Business College Ltd. v. Henderson Secretarial School Ltd.*, [1939] 4 D.L.R. 151 (Alta. C.A.); *Doerner v. Bliss & Laughlin Industries Inc.* (1980), 54 C.P.R. (2d) 1 (S.C.C.); *Denison v. Carrousel Farms Ltd.* (1981), 62 C.P.R. (2d) 28 (Ont. H.C.), affd (1982), 67 C.P.R. (2d) 185 (Ont. C.A.).

[3]   See Chapter 11, "Trade Secrets", for a discussion of the protection of confidential information.

[4]   See, for example, *Garbutt Business College Ltd. v. Henderson Secretarial School Ltd.*, *supra* footnote 2, where a rival college was set up in breach of the covenant.

[5]   See, for example, *Saskatchewan Co-operative Wheat Producers Ltd. v. Zurowski*, *supra*, footnote 2 and *Esso Petroleum Co. v. Harper's Garage (Stourport) Ltd.*, *supra*, footnote 2.

[6]   Where the interests being protected are obligations of confidence, the reasonable period of the restriction might be the head start and advantage which ownership of the confidential information gives to the party.

[7]   Usually the reasonable period is relatively short excluding cases involving sale of businesses or trade secrets. A rule of thumb is that the restraint may not exceed two years. See, however, the case of *Thorsten Nordenfelt v. Maxim Nordenfelt Guns & Ammunition Co.*, [1894] A.C. 535 (H.L.), in which a worldwide and perpetual restriction on competition by the inventor of the maxim machine gun was upheld by the House of Lords. In that case, the restriction was found to be not wider than necessary to protect the purchaser, nor was it injurious to the public.

The restriction must not only meet the requirements above, it must also be reasonable with regard to the public interest. For example, in *Tank Lining Corp. v. Dunlop Industries Ltd.*,[8] a party was bound by a two-year Canada-wide prohibition from engaging in the business of lining tank cars as a term in a licence of confidential information and know-how to the licensee. The licensee ceased making payments under the licence agreement. The Court found the terms reasonable and enforceable and found that there was no social or economic harm to the public as a result of the covenant. The covenant was neutral in so far as the public interest was concerned.

By contrast in *Kores Manufacturing Co. v. Kolok Manufacturing*,[9] the two companies agreed to indefinite covenants not to hire the employees of the other. The Court found the restriction to be grossly exceeding what was adequate to protect manufacturing secrets. The restriction was also unreasonable as it applied to *all* employees, not just employees having the applicable knowledge. This restraint was struck down as being not in the interests of the parties.

---

[8]   (1982), 68 C.P.R. (2d) 162 (Ont. C.A.).

[9]   [1959] 1 Ch. 108 (U.K. C.A.).

Index

[All references are to page numbers of the text.]